"Churches can create a welcoming environment for the unchurched and skeptical but not know what's next. In our parish we've discovered that it is absolutely necessary to communicate to everybody—whether they are a life-long Catholic or not—clear and accessible steps for deepening their faith. This book can help your parish do that and focus on what truly matters."

Fr. Gregory A. Reichlen
Pastor of the Church of St. John
East Stroudsburg, Pennsylvania

"*Rebuilt Faith* is an outstanding, practical, and entertaining handbook that will lead you on a path to renewing your relationship with Jesus. It is easy to read yet rich with wisdom, simple yet thought-provoking, and at times challenging. Following it and applying it daily will lead to personal transformation. You will have a renewed fervor for the Catholic faith and will be led to discover the true desires of your heart."

Stephanie Clancy
Finance Council Chair at Church of the Nativity
Timonium, Maryland

"I have so many incredible things I could say about the work that Fr. Michael White, Tom Corcoran, and their leadership team at Church of the Nativity are doing to change the way that parishes do church. After reading White and Corcoran's first book, *Rebuilt*, and learning about the steps for rebuilding faith now detailed in *Rebuilt Faith*, everything changed for me as a parishioner who became a parish leader. If you are feeling stuck on your faith journey or don't know where to start rebuilding your relationship with Jesus, let these authors guide you! Parish leaders, this is a must-share with your teams, parishioners, small groups, and anyone you know who seeks renewal in their Catholic faith."

Melissa Wilkinson
Pastoral Assoc̲i̲a̲t̲... ̲. Mary's Church
Falls, New York

D1409079

"What a great book! So incredibly needed! Fr. Michael White and Tom Corcoran have already proven that they know how to create a dynamic, life-changing parish experience for those of us who are searching for belonging, truth, and hope. In *Rebuilt Faith*, they continue to use their special sauce, which is listening to us—answering the questions that we are actually asking. We swim in skeptical currents and long for more than a list of rules to follow. We want our lives to change. This is the book to help make that happen. Utterly applicable to daily life, *Rebuilt Faith* is broken down into forty days, which helps reset our crowded minds and create new habits. This book is for you, your questioning friend, your doubting loved one. In these pages, you'll encounter the One—the only One—who has the answers, the hope, and the joy that you are searching for."

Lisa Brenninkmeyer
CEO and founder of Walking with Purpose

"Michael White and Tom Corcoran—these two good shepherds—have done it again! They've written a timely, practical, wise, and humorous book that is sure to help not only skeptics but anyone searching to know the critical questions and the first steps in becoming a disciple of Jesus. The handbook style of this book with its brief teaching content and reflection questions will facilitate both the informing of the mind and the deep searching of the heart that are foundational elements to rebuilding one's faith."

Peter Herbeck
Executive Vice President and Director of Missions
Renewal Ministries

"Fr. Michael White and Tom Corcoran reminded me why Sunday Mass matters: because Jesus, whom I love, is there. If you're seeking Jesus, or just seeking something more in life, this book might be just what you're looking for."

Shannon Wimp Schmidt
Parish Vitality Coordinator
Archdiocese of Chicago

40 Days to Uncover What Matters

rebuilt
FAITH

A Handbook for Skeptical Catholics

Michael White and Tom Corcoran

Foreword by Bishop Adam J. Parker

Ave Maria Press AVE Notre Dame, Indiana

Nihil Obstat: Reverend Monsignor Michael Heintz, PhD
                    Censor Librorum

Imprimatur: Most Reverend Kevin C. Rhoades
                    Bishop of Fort Wayne–South Bend
                    Given at: Fort Wayne, Indiana, on 22 May 2023

Founded in 1865, Ave Maria Press is a ministry of the United States Province of Holy Cross.

www.avemariapress.com

Paperback: ISBN-13 978-1-64680-201-2

E-book: ISBN-13 978-1-64680-202-9

Product number: 30012

Cover images © Unsplash.

Cover and text design by Andy Wagoner.

Library of Congress Cataloging-in-Publication Data is available.

Printed in Canada

To
CAROL "SUE" ABROMAITIS
mentor, friend, and
inspiring witness to Catholic Christianity

Contents

Foreword

When I was ordained a bishop, I chose as my motto "Go make disciples." Jesus spoke those words two thousand years ago to his friends as their clear mission. They are words that continue to ring out as the mission and rallying cry for his Church. The Church exists for this simple purpose of connecting everyone to the person of Jesus Christ.

While a clear mission, it is up to each generation to discern what it means to make disciples in their time. We bishops, together with our brother priests, religious, and lay collaborators, must bring fresh insight into serving our mission given the culture we find ourselves in and the circumstances in which we operate.

Direction is also needed in balancing the importance of personal ownership of faith within the larger community of the Catholic Church. Faith is *personal*, so individuals must choose habits and practices that build their faith. At the same time, faith is not *private*. A healthy, growing faith requires that it be lived within the community of belief and practice that is God's family.

This book offers fresh insights into *how* to live your faith, both personally and in the context of a parish. Whether you're a "cradle Catholic" or new to the Christian life, you'll find this a welcome resource. But the authors clearly have a heart for Catholics who are questioning or no longer practice their faith, a large and growing population in this country. This book will be especially helpful to them. Pastors and parish leaders will also be well advised to introduce programs of parish renewal and evangelization according to the discipleship path described here.

The ideas found in these pages were dreamed up not in a diocesan chancery or consultant's office but in a parish, the community of Church of the Nativity here in the Archdiocese of Baltimore. As I have interacted with the pastor Fr. Michael, whom I have known for many years, and his lay associate and coauthor, Tom, I have repeatedly been impressed by their enthusiasm for making disciples and their continued commitment to shaping a successful discipleship path. This enthusiasm and commitment in turn is reflected in their vibrant and successful parish community, filled with flourishing disciples who have grown precisely by taking the steps you'll find in this book.

Two thousand years ago, the world was changed, transformed, and turned upside down for the good and for God as a critical mass of people decided to follow Jesus and radically commit to loving one another. I believe our country is ready for another such revival led by fully committed Catholics enthusiastic about their faith. This book will help get that revival started.

May God abundantly bless you in this journey.

Bishop Adam J. Parker
Vicar General | Archdiocese of Baltimore
January 1, 2023

Introduction

Wisdom is born of wonder.

—*St. Gregory the Great*

What We're About . . .

The disruption caused by our collective COVID-19 experience accelerated an already well-established pattern of Catholics drifting away from the life of the Church. The "cafeteria" Catholicism of the past four or five decades—in which Catholics would pick and choose which aspects of the Church's teachings and practices they wanted to follow—has become dormant Catholicism for more and more baptized Catholics.

Many have left in protest of some Church teaching they take exception to. Others have departed in disappointment or even despair over the revelations of decades of sexual abuse and cover-ups, which have eroded trust and credibility in the Church. And many more, in our experience, have drifted away out of boredom. They are simply bored with church experiences that are simply boring and often bad: unwelcome, irrelevant distractions to their daily lives filled with far more engaging activities. Sure, most of these people still believe in God and seek to do good and avoid evil. They're just not easily convinced that church matters. They've grown skeptical about Catholicism and doubt that there is any compelling need for alignment with a particular faith tradition or involvement in a religious community. *Really, what's the point?* they wonder.

If any of this describes you (or someone you love) right now, we're glad you're reading! You're *exactly* who we wrote this book for.

What We Want for You . . .

Our goal for this book is to help those who have stopped going
to church entirely or mostly, and those close to leaving, to recon-
sider and rebuild their Catholic faith, though it will also be helpful to those who feel the need to renew or refresh it. In short,
we have written this book for skeptical Catholics, those actively
wondering, *Is religious faith a thing I really need in my life? Does
it really matter? If it does, why am I not more engaged?*

The first part of this book aims at reminding you, in the simplest, most straightforward manner possible, *what* Catholicism is
all about or, rather, *who* it is all about—Jesus Christ and developing a relationship with him as individuals and together in community. Then, we lay out five simple steps anyone can take to
grow in that relationship that we call "faith." Simplicity brings
clarity, and we need clarity to *see* these steps and the motivation
to *take* them. It is our hope that this book helps you gain the
vision and find the motivation.

What we share in the following pages comes from our experience of serving in our suburban parish in Baltimore and walking with people who are growing spiritually. This book is also
shaped by our individual stories of growing closer to God as
increasingly committed yet still deeply flawed disciples of Jesus
Christ.

As we and our parishioners have taken the five steps you'll
find here, we have seen God move from an abstract idea in people's imaginations to a deeply loved partner who provides a far
greater sense of purpose for living than most of us ever had
before.

What We Want from You . . .

This book is laid out in brief daily exercises over the course of
forty days.

Why forty? Forty was the number of years the Israelites wandered in the desert, in punishment for their infidelity. And forty was the number of days Jesus prayed in the desert preparing for his mission. Forty days is also a solid span of time to adopt new habits. So we present forty daily exercises for rebuilding your faith that are intended to be undertaken on *consecutive* days. In other words, rather than racing through these exercises all at once, they're meant to be undertaken *gradually*, even *slowly*, one day at a time.

Each daily exercise will take only about ten minutes to complete. Make it a part of your daily routine: read it with your morning coffee, during your lunch break, or as you relax in the evening. Commit to a time *and* a place. If you don't have the *time*, or if you can't find a quiet *place*, that could be your first step in this process. If you miss a day, push yourself to get back to it the very next day. Consistency is key. In the final week we add two bonus days, just to complete the last week and provide a clear conclusion.

Each day's exercise brings you three tools to help you progress toward a rebuilt faith by reading, reflecting, and rebuilding or building for the first time your relationship with God in Christ Jesus.

- **A Daily Reading:** The reading will help you consider if and how much having a vibrant faith matters to you. This short reading sets the theme or focus for your day.

- **Three Questions for Reflection:** Take a few moments at the end of your quiet time to think about these questions. If a question doesn't make sense or is too easily answered, then move on. If, on the other hand, a question resonates with you, then slow down to ponder it. To get the most out of this book, write out your thoughts; maybe even consider keeping a journal for this exercise. If family or friends are making this journey with you, carve out time for regular conversations on these reflections. You could even form a small discussion, faith-sharing group.

- **A Prayer and a Verse to Help You Rebuild:** The closing prayer at the end of each day summarizes the lesson, helping you lift it to God and also establish a habit of daily prayer. Consider praying out loud, even if quietly. Verbalizing our prayers can increase their impact on us.

Each day's exercise relies on scripture to make our case and tell our story. Some days will examine a passage thoroughly and at length. Others will provide only a brief reference. At the end of each day's exercise comes a verse to remember. Memorizing scripture and repeating it back to yourself in the course of the day can have a powerful effect on your appreciation of the Bible and can motivate you to take your next step in faith.

As you can see, getting the most out of this book depends on your commitment to the daily practice but also on your personal preferences. Some people will want to undertake the whole program and follow the plan in a precise way. Others will inevitably find it more helpful to tailor the daily exercises to fit how they learn and grow. And that is perfectly fine. These exercises are not homework assignments; there will not be a final exam and there are no grades given, so feel free to use what works best for you.

What We Want You to Know . . .

If you started reading this book, it's probably because you're looking for something for yourself or someone you know. And we believe that something is God and a place in the family of faith he forms and nourishes, which we know as the Catholic Church.

We know God has great things in store for you over the next forty days. He can take your faith to a new level, to the *next* level.

You can come to know God's grace, favor, and loving-kindness in a new way, a personal way. We invite and encourage you to make time to uncover for yourself what really matters.

Read.

Reflect.

Rebuild your faith.

WEEK ONE

Get to Know Jesus

DAY 1

Ask the Most Important Question

*For I do not seek to understand in order to believe,
but I believe in order to understand.
For I know this: unless I believe I will not understand.*

—*St. Anselm of Canterbury*

Read

It's all about Jesus.

Rebuilding your Catholic faith begins with that nagging, perhaps aching feeling in your heart for *more*: more connectedness, more community, more purpose. The rebuilding that those feelings can introduce ends with Jesus. That's our experience anyway.

If you're skeptical of the Church because you're mad at the Church or you've just grown bored with religion and its rules, we invite you to keep reading, because faith is not about the Church's missteps and it's not about religious rule keeping. It's about Jesus. He is the cornerstone of faith, the firm foundation of living and growing in faith.

And so, as we begin the process of rebuilding that this book proposes, we start with a question, a basic question, that comes in the Gospel of Matthew. Actually, that basic question is preceded by another question: "When Jesus went into the region of Caesarea Philippi he asked his disciples, 'Who do *people* say that the Son of Man is?'" (Matthew 16:13, emphasis added).

Apparently, *everyone* was talking about him, so the apostles had plenty of answers: "Some say John the Baptist, others Elijah, still others Jeremiah or one of the prophets" (Matthew 16:14). Their answers reveal the conflict and confusion about the person and role of Jesus of Nazareth, as he knew it would. But all the noise sets the stage for that other question. It is the central question of this book. "[Jesus] said to them, 'But who do *you* say that I am?'" (Matthew 16:15, emphasis added).

Who do you say Jesus is? In his book *Between Heaven and Hell*, author Peter Kreeft notes that every human being must fall into *two* of these four categories:

- people who claim to be God
- people who don't claim to be God
- sages
- non-sages

There are people who are *non*-sages and *don't claim to be God*. They are most of the people throughout human history. We assume just about everybody reading this book falls into this category. We definitely do. Then, there are the *non-sages who claim to be God*. These people are either not well or lying.

Next comes the category of the *sage*, a wise person. Historically, there have been many great and wise figures: Confucius, Buddha, Socrates, Plato, Aristotle, Hildegard of Bingen, Catherine of Siena, Julian of Norwich, Teresa of Avila, Gandhi, Thomas Merton, Dorothy Day, and Oprah. Just kidding on Oprah, but here's the point: none of them *claimed to be God*.

Jesus is consistently recognized as a sage throughout the Common Era. Most would easily agree that he offers great, often unique, insight into living. But while other sages could say through study and discernment that they had found the *way*, come to recognize *truth*, or finally figured out *life*, only Jesus said, "I *am* the way and the truth and the life. No one comes to the Father except through me" (John 14:6, emphasis added).

Jesus was the Lord, a liar, or someone suffering from delusions. He didn't leave any other options. So when Jesus asked his followers, "Who do you say that I am?" Simon Peter's possible answers were limited, and he responded, "You are the Messiah, the Son of the living God" (Matthew 16:16).

It's important to note that this is the first time any of the apostles made such a statement. They didn't start out believing Jesus was the Son of God. They had to *come* to believe it. Peter was the first among them to embrace this belief, and Jesus said to him in reply, "Blessed are you, Simon son of Jonah. For flesh and blood has not revealed this to you, but my heavenly Father" (Matthew 16:17).

Jesus tells Simon Peter that he knows Peter has not arrived at his faith on his own; he's just not smart enough. He had inspiration from God the Father. But the truth is that none of us is that smart. We all need help in coming to faith in Jesus. Faith is called a *theological virtue*, meaning it is a *gift* from God. We can choose whether or not to receive the gift, but it is a gift. That's why it doesn't make any sense for someone who has received faith in Jesus to judge those who haven't.

Within the community of the Church, we have to answer the question of who Jesus is *objectively*, but that's not enough. Jesus does not mean for the question to be an abstract one. It's intended as a deeply personal and *subjective* one, and one we return to often. It is a question to be worked out in every area of our lives. So, as we begin this journey, ask the Father to help you draw closer to his Son and reveal who he is in your life. Then ask Jesus to help you follow him.

Reflect

How do you know someone is wise?

Who are people you respect for their wisdom?

Why does Jesus's wisdom stand out in human history?

Rebuild

God, our heavenly Father,
reveal to me the truth about your Son
who he is and who he can be in my life.
I want to get to know him better.
I desire a closer relationship with him.
During these forty days, strengthen my resolve,
and give me courage to believe.
I pray through Christ our Lord.
Amen.

[Jesus] said to them, "But who do you
say that I am?"

—Matthew 16:15

DAY 2

Ask the (Second) Most Important Question

You have made us for yourself and our heart is restless until it rests in you.

—St. Augustine

Read

The most important question is "Who is Jesus in my life?" That bids the second most important question, "Is the effort to follow him worth it?"

We all follow something or someone in pursuit of wholeness and happiness. Some people make money and possessions the foundation of their lives. They focus most of their energy on building their net worth. Some people follow fame, achievement, and *success*. If they can gain celebrity as an actor or athlete, respect as a business leader, or influence as a political figure, then they believe they will be happy and find meaning. Some people set pleasure as their goal. They go from party to party, experience to experience, and relationship to relationship, believing that feeling good and having fun are worth giving their lives to. Some people are just addicted to power. And, of course, some people want it all.

Possessions, popularity, pleasure, power—they call us to follow, pursuing the happiness we all desire. But what they all reveal is actually a fundamental truth—that we instinctively know we need something outside of ourselves to be satisfied, to feel complete. In that way, we are not unlike a man Jesus met on one of his journeys.

Here is how the encounter went: "Now someone approached him and said, 'Teacher, what good must I do to gain eternal life?'" (Matthew 19:16).

We know from the other gospel accounts of the same story that this guy wasn't exactly lacking in worldly ways. Luke tells us he was a "ruler," a person of position and power over others. Mark's gospel includes the details that he was rich and young. In other words, he has it all: possessions, popularity, pleasure, and power. And yet, apparently, it isn't enough. It doesn't fulfill him.

We've all been let down by someone, or something, probably lots of things. And when that person or that thing fails to deliver on our expectations, we lie to ourselves that it is only a question of a little bit more: another new shiny object, a longer vacation, a girlfriend who really understands me, a husband who actually listens, and then we'll be happy. Howard Hughes, an American business mogul and film producer, was asked how much money it takes to make a man happy, and he answered, "Just a little bit more."

The young man calls Jesus "Teacher" because he believes Jesus has something to teach him about life, and not just *this* life but *eternal* life. And his question is a pretty important one, isn't it? If you believe in heaven, you very much want to know what you have to do, what good deeds must be undertaken, to get in. However, that's only one part of the question. Hearing the phrase "eternal life," we tend to think of what happens *after* death. But when the gospels refer to eternal life, it is a reference to *quality of life* that can be experienced right now, as well as the life to come.

And Jesus replied, "If you wish to enter into life, keep the commandments" (Matthew 19:17). This is an entirely predictable, completely pedestrian answer, just what you would expect. And the text doesn't say this, but perhaps Jesus started to walk

away and move on with his journey, so unimportant, so insignificant seemed the exchange. Besides, certainly there were other
people seeking his attention and other questions being asked.
Just as if you were out walking or on a run and someone asked
you for directions, you probably would answer as you go.

But this guy would not give up: "He asked him, 'Which ones?'
And Jesus replied, "'You shall not kill; you shall not commit adultery; you shall not steal; you shall not bear false witness; honor
your father and mother"; and "you shall love your neighbor as
yourself""" (Matthew 19:18–19).

The man wants additional details, specific instructions. Is
he living out all the commandments that will get him happiness
here as well as get him home to heaven? So Jesus recites the basic
ones. It is still an entirely shallow answer, really basic stuff that
any school child could have repeated. It didn't take any spiritual
insight to know that you need to avoid murder. In fact, Jesus's
answer seems cliché, rather weak coming from someone who
is supposed to be a great teacher. However, far from shallow,
Jesus shrewdly leads this man deeper into the discussion. Does
he really want to lean into the question of what *he* needs to do
to find the life he's looking for? And, it turns out, he does. He
presses Jesus, "All these I have observed; what do I still lack?"
(Matthew 19:20).

This young man acknowledges he's done everything religious
law dictates and has found it unsatisfying. Just as his wealth has
failed to fulfill him, he knows there has to be more than following the rules and staying out of trouble, as these too have failed to
fulfill him. His heart aches to experience something of the eternal that has up to this point eluded him.

Maybe, like this rich young ruler, you've tried the kind of
religion that is all about religious rule keeping. Perhaps you've
associated Catholicism with just keeping your nose clean, obey-
ing the commandments, and checking the proper boxes. You
fulfilled your obligations, but like this man, you have come to

understand there has to be more to faith than legalism. Maybe you walked away from church because the whole exercise just felt rote, shallow, and irrelevant to your life.

Like you, this guy is looking for more, and Jesus gives it to him. Jesus said to him, "If you wish to be perfect, go, sell what you have and give to [the] poor, and you will have treasure in heaven. Then come, follow me" (Matthew 19:21).

The Gospel of Mark includes the telling detail that before Jesus told this man to give away his possessions, he looked at him and loved him (Mark 10:21a). Jesus loves the guy and loves that he is in search of the more his heart aches for. And he loves him enough to pause in his journey and tell this guy the truth: "If you want to find the fulfillment you seek, you've got to follow me, and for *you,* following me means giving up your wealth." However, this passage is not about money; it's about the man. And in *his* case, following Jesus also meant parting with his wealth.

"When the young man heard this statement, he went away sad, for he had many possessions" (Matthew 19:22). Notice the guy does not leave happy. He doesn't go skipping merrily back to embrace his possessions. He goes away sad because he knows exactly what he will be going back to: more of the unsatisfying sameness of his life. He goes away sad because he does not want to do what is most *needed* to achieve what is most *desired.*

Can we do what is most needed to achieve what is most desired? And why should we? Is it worth it?

Reflect

What have you pursued over and over again, thinking that it would fill the ache in your heart for happiness but instead has consistently left you unfulfilled?

What have you invested in heavily—an opportunity,
a relationship, or an ongoing activity—that ultimately
disappointed?

If you say that Jesus is Lord, how can you show in your
actions, pursuits, or decisions that he really can fulfill your
longing for more?

Rebuild

Oh God, you know my mind and my heart.
Send your Holy Spirit to enlighten me
about the choices I make and the values I hold.
Awaken within me the desire for eternity that you have
placed in my heart. I pray through Christ our Lord.
Amen.

When the young man heard this statement,
he went away sad,
for he had many possessions.

—Matthew 19:22

DAY 3

Earn Rewards

We have found the Messiah!

—*St. Andrew*

Read

The rich young ruler walks away from Jesus. He goes back to the same life he found unfulfilling because he cannot put aside his money even for a better life, prompting Jesus to turn to his disciples and say, "It will be hard for one who is rich to enter the kingdom of heaven" (Matthew 19:23).

This is not a judgment; it is an insight about human nature. The comment is made not with condescension but with sadness and regret. If you have any kind of worldly wealth, if you enjoy significant popularity, pleasures, or power, or if you're all about the pursuit of fame and fortune, it can be difficult to remain open to the gifts of the kingdom of heaven. There's certainly nothing wrong with possessions, popularity, pleasure, or power. In fact, they can be signs to us of God's goodness and reminders of the more he has in store for us. But here's a truth we need to recognize: we can easily set our hearts on passing things, temporary things, rather than the eternal things, and in doing so, we separate our hearts from God's love.

Because this was a completely unexpected teaching, Jesus's friends are skeptical. So, he repeats it, with added emphasis. "Again, I say to you, it is easier for a camel to pass through the

17

eye of a needle than for one who is rich to enter the kingdom of God" (Matthew 19:24).

A camel is a huge animal, one of the biggest. The eye of a needle is about as small a slit as the naked eye can see. Passing a camel through a needle's eye would be absurd to even consider. So what is Jesus talking about? Is he automatically excluding from paradise anyone lucky enough to live well? Not at all. Jesus says this so that the disciples will understand the utter futility of thinking *any* human effort, on its own, will get them into God's kingdom. Jesus makes this pronouncement for its shock value. And it works. "When the disciples heard this, they were greatly astonished and said, 'Who then can be saved?'" (Matthew 19:25).

For the early disciples, like everyone in that culture, wealth was evidence that you were favored by God. Money was proof positive not only that God loved you but also that he loved you *more* than he loved other people. If it was impossible for the wealthy, blessed by God in life, to get into heaven, then no one really had a shot.

That they expected to be rich themselves was a further cause for astonishment. Believing Jesus was the long-awaited Messiah and one day he would be king, the disciples assumed they would be swept into power along with him and obviously enjoy all the trappings of their new offices. They're left wondering if there is any hope for them. "Jesus looked at them and said, 'For human beings this is impossible, but for God all things are possible'" (Matthew 19:26).

The teaching here is simple: You can't gain eternal life on your own effort. You can't even earn your way there by a track record of good deeds. Neither can you buy your way in. Following the religious rule book and checking all the boxes won't work for you either. We have access to salvation through Christ alone. We need a savior. But even so, our Savior asks us to follow him and serve him, and that service requires sacrifice. The question remains: Is it worth it?

Peter speaks up for the group and impulsively asks the question that's on everybody's mind. "Then Peter said to him in reply, 'We have given up everything and followed you. What will there be for us?'" (Matthew 19:27). Peter watches the rich young ruler walk away from Jesus and thinks, "Wait a minute. I did what that guy couldn't do. I left everything for you, Jesus: a very successful fishing business and time with my friends and family, to follow you on this journey. What's in it for me?"

Over and over in his preaching and teaching Jesus tells his friends and followers that to be his disciples they will have to make sacrifices. And, in fact, at this point in the story, they already have, as Peter points out. Again, the question is, will it be worth it?

We will see this more in the days ahead, but most often Jesus pointed to the *rewards* of following him. Repeatedly he tells the disciples to follow because in the end it will be worth it. The promise includes short-term benefits as well as lasting, long-term ones. Here's what he says to Peter: "Amen, I say to you that you who have followed me, in the new age, when the Son of Man is seated on his throne of glory, will yourselves sit on twelve thrones, judging the twelve tribes of Israel. And everyone who has given up houses or brothers or sisters or father or mother or children or lands for the sake of my name will receive a hundred times more, and will inherit eternal life" (Matthew 19:28–29).

Jesus tells the apostles in the "new age," when this world has passed away, they will rule over Israel. That was his promise to them. Everyone else, and that can include us, who has sacrificed possessions, popularity, pleasure, or power to follow the Lord will receive a hundred times *more* than they gave up. It's an exchange, and it is an incredibly generous exchange.

Will it be difficult to follow Jesus at times? Will it require service and sacrifice? Of course. Will you lose out on some things others will have? Probably. Will it be worth it? Definitely. Follow him, and you will be glad you did.

Reflect

What were you taught about Jesus and what it means to follow him?

Do you consider yourself to be a Christ follower? What might the Lord be asking you to give up in order to follow him more closely?

Do you believe in Jesus's promise of rewards? Why or why not?

Rebuild

God, heavenly Father,
Help me to see that the rewards of serving Jesus
are greater than the temporary joys
of all that distract me from following him.
I pray in Jesus's name.
Amen.

And everyone who has given up
houses or brothers or sisters or father
or mother or children or lands for the
sake of my name will receive a hundred
times more, and will inherit eternal life.

—Matthew 19:29

DAY 4

Meet the Man

Behold the Lamb of God who takes away the sins of the world.

—*St. John the Baptist*

Read

> **Tom:** I've developed a shorthand phrase to describe someone I've just met who seems interesting, someone I would enjoy getting to know better. I say "I'd have a beer with him." Don't get me wrong, beer isn't an indispensable element in making new friends (although sometimes it helps). It just suggests the comfortable experience of getting to know someone who is worth pursuing as a friend.

So is Jesus a guy you would want to have a beer with? Is Jesus likable? Would you want to spend time with him? These types of questions don't get raised often enough when it comes to following Jesus, at least not in the Catholic settings we've been part of. Jesus doesn't ask us to follow him out of mere obligation or merely for the rewards. He invites us to follow him, but he doesn't just want *followers*; he's looking for *friends*: people who really come to know him, like him, and develop a personal relationship with him as a result.

At one point Jesus says, "I no longer call you slaves because a slave does not know what his master is doing. I have called

21

you friends" (John 15:15). Jesus, whom we profess to be the Son of God, desires friendship with us. Talk about friends in high places.

What is friendship? Many definitions can be cited. Simply stated, friendship is appreciation based on knowledge and experience of another person. It means knowing someone uniquely. Our friends are simply people we like to be with.

So is Jesus likable? Do you like Jesus? To really build, or rebuild, our Catholic faith, we have to increase our appreciation of Jesus's style and personality. We can do that by looking at three stories that show us different aspects of his character.

Instructive and Playful

"When they came to Capernaum, the collectors of the temple tax approached Peter and said, 'Doesn't your teacher pay the temple tax?'" (Matthew 17:24).

Every man twenty years of age and older was required to pay a tax for the upkeep and support of the Temple in Jerusalem. Here, the officials in charge question Peter if Jesus intends to pay his fair share. That Peter responds in the affirmative is somewhat humorous because he had no idea if Jesus was going to pay the tax, as the story eventually makes clear. Peter returns home only to discover Jesus already knows what's going on: "When he came into the house, before he had time to speak, Jesus . . . said to him, '. . . Go to the sea, drop in a hook, and take the first fish that comes up. Open its mouth and you will find a coin worth twice the temple tax. Give that to them for me and for you,'" (Matthew 17:25–27).

Jesus could have paid the tax in any way he chose, but he approaches the moment, which the tax collectors had presented with such gravitas, with whimsy and playfulness. He tells Peter, who is a fisherman, to go fishing and discover, in the mouth of his catch, a coin to pay the tax! It is all rather fantastical and underscores his creativity. He turns a rather prosaic exercise (what could be more prosaic than paying your taxes?) into a game.

Unexpected and Unconventional

"As Jesus passed on from there, he saw a man named Matthew sitting at the customs post. He said to him, 'Follow me.' And he got up and followed him. While he was at the table in his house, many tax collectors and sinners came and sat with Jesus and his disciples" (Matthew 9:9–10).

Jesus invites Matthew, a tax collector, to follow him. Caravaggio's painting *The Calling of St. Matthew* perfectly captures the utterly shocking nature of this call. In Caravaggio's interpretation, Jesus points at Matthew as if to say, "It's you," as Matthew points to the guy next to him as if to say, "How about him?" As we will see, tax collectors were considered the lowest of the low in that society. But Jesus overturns this long-held view with a simple call for Matthew to follow. Then, Jesus further disrupts the established order of things by going to Matthew's house to eat with all his tax collector friends.

Jesus attends a party . . . with sinners! One of the accusations the religious leaders consistently made against Jesus was that he was a glutton and a drunkard. And it was because of scenes like this one, in which he was not afraid to have a good time and enjoy social gatherings. Neither was he in the least reluctant to hang around with people who thought and lived very differently than he did. And, it turned out, people who were nothing like him liked him.

The Pharisees, though, "saw this and said to his disciples, 'Why does your teacher eat with tax collectors and sinners?' [Jesus] heard this and said, 'Those who are well do not need a physician, but the sick do. Go and learn the meaning of the words, "I desire mercy, not sacrifice." I did not come to call the righteous but sinners'" (Matthew 9:11–13). Woah! That's a major burn. Jesus tells the Pharisees, who were considered the nation's

primary and most prestigious teachers, that they need to go back
to school for a reeducation in the ways of God. He calls them
self-righteous because they had lost sight of God's goodness and
their own need for his mercy. In this sense, Jesus was a rebel. He
rebels against the status quo. Unexpectedly, unconventionally, he
challenges leaders who lose sight of the reason for their position
and authority. We love this about Jesus.

Simply Brilliant and Entirely Disarming

"Then the Pharisees went off and plotted how they might entrap
him in speech. They sent their disciples to him, with the Herodians, saying, 'Teacher, we know that you are a truthful man. . . .
Tell us, then, what is your opinion: Is it lawful to pay the census
tax to Caesar or not?'" (Matthew 22:15–17).

Again and again we see the plotting of the religious leaders
who were jealous of Jesus's popularity. The Pharisees plot with
the Herodians, secular Jewish leaders associated with the court
of the king. These two groups did not usually agree on anything,
but they both find Jesus to be a problem and want him out of
the way. So they devise a plot to trip him up and trap him. They
question him about *another* tax, the Roman tax.

Of course, taxes are never popular, but this one was despised.
Constantly and cruelly, the tax reminded the Jewish people that
they were subjected to Roman rule. The money went straight
into the Roman emperor's coffers. The Jewish people were fund-
ing his unbridled power, extravagant luxury, and decadent lifestyle as they eked out an existence in poverty and oppression.
Furthermore, the tax had to be paid with Roman coinage that
bore the engraving of the emperor and an inscription basically
naming Caesar a god. The tax represented a profound insult to
the Jewish people not only politically but also religiously. Using
the coin was a form of idolatry to the pious Jew.

Jesus seems trapped in a no-win situation. Affirm the tax, and he looks like a traitor to his countrymen. Deny it, and the Romans will arrest him for sedition. What to do?

Jesus says to them, "'Why are you testing me, you hypocrites? Show me the coin that pays the census tax.' Then they handed him the Roman coin" (Matthew 22:18–19). In asking them to show him the coin, Jesus exposes the whole exchange for the theater that it was, rather than a sincere inquiry regarding religious practice. How? By producing the coin, his enemies reveal themselves as artless hypocrites. They relied upon the coin in their own transactions, just like everyone else. They walk right into the trap they set for him. Take a look at how he closes it: "'Whose image is this and whose inscription?' They replied, 'Caesar's.' At that he said to them, 'Then repay to Caesar what belongs to Caesar and to God what belongs to God.' When they heard this they were amazed" (Matthew 22:20–22).

Simply brilliant! His answer fields their question in a way that amazes and astonishes his opponents and delights his friends. Entirely avoiding their trap, Jesus leaves them disarmed. He can be accused neither of inciting rebellion nor of contradicting God's claim on our hearts.

We love Jesus's style. Beyond the sacrifices and rewards, he's definitely someone worth spending time with.

Reflect

Do you like Jesus? Why or why not?

What are your thoughts on having a friendship with Jesus?

What are the character traits of people you like? Do you think Jesus shares these same traits?

Rebuild

God, our heavenly Father,
grant me the grace to truly appreciate your Son, Jesus,
and to grow in friendship with him.
In his holy name.
Amen.

[Jesus said,] "I no longer call you slaves,
because a slave does not know what his
master is doing. I have called you friends."

—John 15:15

DAY 5

And Get to Know Him

He who was the Son of God became the Son of
man, that men might become sons of God.

—*St. Irenaeus of Lyon*

Read

Despite the Church's exclusively all male hierarchy and priest-
hood, in many places around the world—most certainly in the
United States—the overwhelming percentage of parish staff
are women. And women far outnumber men when it comes
to church attendance. It is not at all uncommon for the parish
weekend Masses to feature women in nearly every possible role
aside from the priest-celebrant; they are the lectors, cantors,
choir members and musicians, altar servers, ushers, and eucharistic ministers. We acknowledge these facts with all due appreciation for the invaluable contribution of women to the life of
Catholic parishes. However, as a result, parishes are often seen as
the province of women.

We do not think it a generalization or an overstatement to
acknowledge that sometimes the experience of church, with
sweetly sentimental music and merely comforting preaching, is
not always attractive to men. For many men, and women too,
the sum total of this kind of church experience is simply boring.

The problem isn't limited to the liturgy. In the broader religious culture, oftentimes Jesus is not portrayed as a man of
power and strength. Much devotional art suggests Jesus to be a

figure of gentleness and kindness but too often in a wholly banal way. Accompanied by little children, he appears as a Mr. Rogers–type figure (minus the cardigan). Many times, these depictions are intended to make Jesus appear accessible, but despite their good intentions, they often form a disappointing or even negative impression.

Popular culture can also suggest that Jesus is gentle to the point of weakness. That, in turn, can shape thoughts and feelings about Christianity and, most definitely, the Church. Who wants to be in a club for losers?

Throughout history the greatest leaders, the most effective leaders, from Joan of Arc to Mother Teresa, from Charlemagne to Churchill, projected strength, clarity, and courage: strength of character, clarity of vision, and courage in their convictions. A "buddy" Jesus who offers quiet support but nothing more might provide encouragement, but he hardly represents a leader worth following. The gospels present a very different figure, one who exhibits that strength of leadership.

Think about it: for most of his life Jesus worked as a carpenter, apprenticing for Joseph. It was a skilled trade, but it also involved hard labor. He no doubt developed calluses on his hands from wielding the tools of his trade. It is easy to imagine, given this background and the subsequent and ceaseless road trips he undertook on foot during his public ministry, often ten to twenty miles a day, that he must have been in great shape.

His physical strength most certainly would have been apparent to the apostles. So much so that they eventually came to believe he was going to lead a military uprising to overthrow the Roman army, even though that army was one of the most powerful military forces in human history. The apostles must have seen a man of strength and power.

There is one event that effectively illustrates our point. It seems that it made such an impression on the apostles that it appears in all four gospels: "Since the Passover of the Jews was near, Jesus went up to Jerusalem" (John 2:13). While observant Jewish people would attend their local synagogue for a weekly celebration of the Sabbath, those able to would go to the Temple in Jerusalem at Passover. Josephus, a Roman historian of Israel living in the gospel period, writes that Jerusalem's population would often swell to include more than two million pilgrims for the annual celebration, an unfathomable crowd for a city the size of ancient Jerusalem. Here, Jesus joined the crowd: "He found in the temple area those who sold oxen, sheep, and doves, as well as the money-changers seated there" (John 2:14). In the courtyard, outside the sanctuary, a robust commercial exchange had sprung up to take advantage of the presence of all the visitors. Specifically, animals were being sold and money exchanged. *Why?*

The pilgrims were coming to worship. And worship and sacrifice went together, as they do in every major religion. At the Temple the faithful would sacrifice oxen, sheep, or doves, depending on their financial means. The sale of sacrificial animals in the Temple precincts was a convenience for those traveling, who could hardly bring their own sacrifice with them. It was also a cash bonanza for the Temple leaders who enjoyed a monopoly and could impose ridiculously inflated prices.

Besides the sale of animals, there were money exchanges. Cash offerings could be made, but Roman coins, with their pagan depictions of the god-emperor, could *not* be used. Instead, Temple coins were required, conveniently only on sale at the Temple with a hefty markup.

It was a scene of crowded, probably cacophonous commerce inconsistent with the grandeur of the sacred space and the solemnity of worship. It was also an environment in which people were being cheated, in the name of God. Stepping into the scene, Jesus quickly becomes angry. That's not an emotion we often associate with him. Growing in our understanding of Jesus is to come to recognize he experienced emotions we experience, including anger and frustration.

Tom: You can learn a great deal about people by knowing what angers them. Their anger
reveals their values and priorities. Recently, I
made a list of my pet peeves at home. They
included

- finding empty milk cartons in the fridge,
- stepping on Legos left scattered on the
  living room floor, and
- leaving the leash on the dog after walking
  him (literally a pet peeve).

The problem with *my* pet peeves is that
they are all about *me*. In each instance (and
believe me, there are plenty of others), I am
frustrated because others (my kids) are making my life more difficult.

Jesus becomes angry here but *not* for selfish or self-centered reasons. He grows angry and then displays his anger for
two selfless reasons. First, the merchants and money changers
(and ultimately the religious leaders who were the big winners in
this commercial enterprise) were essentially extorting the faithful. Second, the Temple court was the only place where Gentiles (non-Jewish people) could come and pray. They were not
allowed inside the Temple itself, yet the one area they *could* use
was an impossible environment to pray in given the commercial
activity.

When you get to the core of what angered Jesus, over and
over again, you find the same thing: corrupt religious leadership.
And what made him angriest of all was when that leadership got
in the way of the faithful connecting with their heavenly Father,
keeping them from knowledge of God's love and mercy, which
those religious leaders' rules and laws tended to do.

Jesus gets angry, and then he *expresses* his anger: "He made a whip out of cords and drove them all out of the temple area, with the sheep and the oxen, and spilled the coins of the money changers and overturned their tables, and to those who sold doves he said, 'Take these out of here, and stop making my Father's house a marketplace'" (John 2:15–16).

Jesus takes in the scene and decides to act boldly. He finds ropes or cords, probably used for the livestock, and fashions them into a whip. With it, he begins driving out the sheep and oxen, no chore for the faint of heart. It is easy to imagine that this small stampede created mayhem in the crowd. Next, he overturns the tables of the money changers: gold and silver flying everywhere. This, in turn, would have sent everyone diving after all those loose coins. In short, Jesus provokes total disruption.

He acts with fierce intentionality, but not with randomness, recklessness, or unkindness. As scholars point out, in the midst of the fury there is no suggestion that any of the animals were hurt; he even displays touching tenderness toward the caged doves, instructing that their cages simply be removed. Over the whole scene he makes the resounding demand, "Stop making *my* Father's house a marketplace" (John 2:16, emphasis added).

"*My* Father's house." Jesus takes the treatment of the Temple personally. His zeal for his Father's house compels him to act, and he does so with passion and purpose, clearly driven by his convictions. In this scene he is a commanding, towering figure, demanding no less than a new order of things.

If we start getting bored with Jesus, we can be sure of this much: whoever we think we're following, it's not Jesus of Nazareth. Jesus never bored anyone. He engaged, taught, fed, and led people. Oftentimes he amazed and astonished them. And sometimes he changed the world as they knew it. That can be our experience too when we take time to really get to know him.

Reflect

When have you been bored in church? When have you been distracted in prayer?

What about church or prayer do you find boring? Why?

Growing up, what images did you have of Jesus of Nazareth?

Rebuild

God, our heavenly Father,
you have given us Jesus as a man of strength,
a leader worth following.
I seek to know his strength and discipline
and emulate his powerful sense of purpose.
Teach me the ways of your Son,
through whom we pray.
Amen.

His disciples recalled the words of scripture,
"Zeal for your house will consume me."

—John 2:17, referencing Psalm 69:10

DAY 6

Find Help

Act and God will act.

—*St. Joan of Arc*

Read

Jesus invites us to follow him, but why should we accept that invitation? Throughout this week we have been looking at *reasons* to follow him. So far, we have learned how Jesus stands out in human history as the only sage who claimed to be the Son of God. As a sage, he speaks truth. As God, he gives life. We've looked at the cost versus the benefits of following Jesus. And it turns out that one of the clearest and most consistent promises he makes concerns the rewards that come in return for discipleship: rewards, he states, that are far in excess of any investment we make. His character, as we noted, is multidimensional, which makes him a fascinating figure. Jesus is kind and compassionate but also clever, playful, and shrewd; he is a man of strength and conviction. Finally, it's easy to follow people we like, and it turns out he's entirely likeable. So we have to ask ourselves the question: Do we like him?

After we answer that question, an equally important question arises: Does he like us? We've noted that he calls us his friends, but does he really *like* us? For that matter, does he even *notice* us? It's not a question Catholics often ask, while inadvertently acting as if he *doesn't*. We adopt the view that God has better things to do than concern himself with us. So let's take a closer look at that. In the passage we're looking at, Jesus and his disciples are on one of their road trips: "They came to Jericho. And as he was leaving Jericho with his disciples and a sizable crowd, Bartimaeus, a blind man, the son of Timaeus, sat by the roadside begging" (Mark 10:46).

Jesus and his apostles traveled through Jericho on their way to Jerusalem. Even two thousand years ago, Jericho was considered an ancient city. Today, archeology reveals evidence of settlements dating back to at least 10,000 BC, making it one of the oldest cities on earth. In visiting Jericho, Jesus is literally passing through history.

Scripture tells us Jesus attracted a *sizable crowd*; other translations refer to a *great multitude*. At this point, near the end of his life, he was phenomenally popular among the people. The juxtaposition of the man of the moment visiting one of the most ancient cities is an interesting one as well. But amid this striking scene, we are introduced to a minor figure of no importance whatsoever.

Bartimaeus was not in the crowd. He couldn't quite navigate the crowd; he was blind. Instead, he sat by the side of the road waiting for the crowd to pass by, providing his very best chance of the day to beg. As a blind man in that culture, begging was how he made a living. There was no trade he could undertake or anything else he could do, and, of course, there was no safety net in society to provide him welfare and relief. All alone and on his own, begging was his only option. But helpless as Bartimaeus was, blind though he might be, he recognizes an opportunity when it literally comes his way.

"On hearing that it was Jesus of Nazareth, he began to cry out and say, 'Jesus, son of David, have pity on me'" (Mark 10:47). Bartimaeus catches the energy and excitement created by Jesus's rock star celebrity, and he wants to be part of it all. At the very least, he can enjoy the largesse of the crowd as they pass by. But, if the stories were true about what this Jesus of Nazareth could do, this could be a life-changing moment. Either way, he gives it a shot.

"And many rebuked him, telling him to be silent. But he kept calling out all the more, 'Son of David, have pity on me'" (Mark 10:48). Of course, everyone wanted Jesus's attention, so many are quick to dissuade and discourage Bartimaeus. How often is that the case? We just want problems and people *with problems* and *problem people* to go away. But Bartimaeus doesn't care about the crowd. He doubles down and calls out all the louder. And it works. "Jesus stopped and said, 'Call him'" (Mark 10:49a). He got Jesus's attention. Jesus paused and instructed his disciples to call the beggar.

"So they called the blind man, saying to him, 'Take courage; get up, he is calling you'" (Mark 10:49). The fickle crowd that was chastising and marginalizing poor Bartimaeus one moment now becomes his cheering section. Bartimaeus, for his part, remained consistent and, more importantly, *persistent,* and it paid off. He'd won a hearing.

"He threw aside his cloak, sprang up, and came to Jesus" (Mark 10:50). This appears to be a small, seemingly insignificant detail, but it is not. Bartimaeus's cloak served as the mainstay of his livelihood. Bartimaeus begged by the busy city gate. Those responding positively would toss coins in his general direction as they passed by. The point of the cloak was to catch the coins, which Bartimaeus could then collect. Throwing the cloak aside, with no assurance that he could ever retrieve it or any previously collected coins, was a tremendous act of faith in the power of Jesus to help him. Bartimaeus doesn't allow his disadvantages or disabilities—or even good things like the coins he has collected—to get in the way of meeting Jesus. He perseveres, knowing this is his chance for a life change, a possible turning point.

"Jesus said to him in reply, 'What do you want me to do for you?'" (Mark 10:51a). This seems a fairly unnecessary question from Jesus. The guy is blind. Jesus has a reputation as a miracle worker. Bartimaeus wants a miracle. Why the question?

However, Jesus often asks this question of people who petition him. He invites the petitioner to explain *why* they are approaching him. When we state our need to Jesus, we are acknowledging that he can actually do something about it. And articulating our needs can help us recognize Jesus's power when he does act. More on that on Day 33.

Here's how Bartimaeus answered Jesus's question: "Master, I want to see." In response, "Jesus told him, 'Go your way; your faith has saved you.' Immediately he received his sight" (Mark 10:51–52).

As soon as Bartimaeus expresses his need, Jesus heals him, giving him sight. Jesus pronounces healing, and just like that, his words have an instant effect. So often, that is the way with Jesus. He slows us down to make us think, to help us reflect on what he can do. And *then*, what he can do, he does in a moment. A problem that was impossible and insurmountable is simply removed.

Jesus heals Bartimaeus and tells him to go on his way. In other words, he said, "Live your life. You have a new beginning; go and make the most of it." He could have told Bartimaeus he owed him, that he expected some kind of return or repayment, perhaps undying gratitude if nothing else. Instead, he grants him full permission to live whatever kind of life he wants. And look what happens: "[He] followed him on the way" (Mark 10:52b). The beauty and simplicity of the verse are worth noting. Bartimaeus chooses to follow Jesus. He doesn't just present himself before the Lord for healing and then take off. His newly gained sight includes a spiritual vision into who Jesus is and what he is about. And so, he follows Jesus's "way." This was the original term for Christians, followers of *the Way*. They were following Jesus, who offered a whole new way of doing life.

As we will explore more tomorrow, following Jesus is a journey in which we integrate his ways into our life. But for now, consider this: Today may be your day, your once-in-a-lifetime opportunity to come to Jesus. It might be your day to approach him, for him to change your life. It might be your day to see Jesus move in a new and exciting way. Do not let this day pass without asking Jesus to come into your life and reveal himself to you, as your friend who knows you and loves you.

Reflect

In what areas of your life do you have trouble "seeing" things clearly or knowing the way forward that's right for you?

Who are the voices in your life discouraging you, and who are the voices encouraging you?

What do you want Jesus to do for you today? How confident are you that he cares and really can help?

Rebuild

God, our heavenly Father,
today, I am choosing to follow your Son.
Like blind Bartimaeus, I want to stand and walk with Jesus and more closely follow his way. I pray this in his name.
Amen.

Jesus told him, "Go your way; your faith has saved you." Immediately he received his sight and followed him on the way.

—Mark 10:52

DAY 7

Take the Right Steps

First do the necessary, then do the feasible,
then you will be able to achieve the impossible.

—*St. Francis of Assisi*

Read

Rebuilding our Catholic faith is all about Jesus. It is all about Jesus and where he *leads us*.

Jesus summed up discipleship (following him) in two statements known individually as the Great Commandment and the Great Commission. At one point, a teacher of the Law approached him to ask which was the greatest commandment in all the Hebrew Scriptures, which Christians call the Old Testament. This question was a hotly debated one at the time, and the lawyer who posed it did so to trap Jesus and trip him up. With 613 laws, it seemed impossible to choose the most important. However, the question didn't faze Jesus at all. Instead, he answered, "You shall love the Lord, your God, with all your heart, with all your soul, and with all your mind. This is the greatest and the first commandment" (Matthew 22:37–38, referencing Deuteronomy 6:4–5).

The prayer Jesus references is found in the book of Deuteronomy and is known as the "Shema." It is the basic confession of Jewish faith made up of three scriptural texts that form the essential part of daily worship. It is a prayer that is ingrained in every Jewish man and woman from childhood. The words would have evoked deep emotions in Jesus's listeners, such as hearing a favorite Christmas carol or singing the national anthem might in us. So important was this prayer that pious Jews hoped the Shema would be their final words before dying.

When Jesus quoted Deuteronomy, everyone probably nodded their heads in agreement. It would have cut through all the debates, dismissing the pettiness and the politics of the day to confirm something Jesus and the Pharisees profoundly held in common. However, Jesus did not stop there, he went on: "The second is like it: You shall love your neighbor as yourself. The whole law and the prophets depend on these two commandments" (Matthew 22:39–40, referencing Leviticus 19:18).

Jesus said you can't separate the love of God from the love of your neighbor. He references Leviticus, which teaches love of neighbor as not only a fundamental command of Jewish law but also one intrinsically yoked to the overarching command to love God. This is what makes Judaism and Christianity so radically different from the pagan religions of ancient times. The pagan gods just wanted your sacrifices and subservience; they didn't care how you treated other people. Judaism, and subsequently Christianity, taught that God our Father cares deeply about both.

Following Jesus means loving God and loving others. That's the Great Commandment.

This, in turn, leads inevitably to the Great Commission. Before Jesus ascended into heaven, he said to his followers: "All power in heaven and on earth has been given to me. Go, therefore, and make disciples of all nations, baptizing them in the name of the Father, and of the Son, and of the holy Spirit, teaching them to observe all that I have commanded you" (Matthew 28:18–20). This command amplifies the instruction to love others. Specifically, we are to love others by helping form them, in the many ways we can do that, as disciples or students of Jesus. It is not enough to simply follow the Lord ourselves; we must help others onto the discipleship path as well (see Day 36).

Following Jesus means living the Great Commandment *and* the Great Commission. To follow Jesus, we must love God, love others, and make disciples. It is that simple *and* that challenging. We like to say that following Jesus is not *easy*, but it can be *simple*.

By "simple" we do not mean simplistic, nor do we suggest an anti-intellectual approach. The Church has a rich intellectual tradition that has yielded a vast treasury of philosophical and theological thought which should always be honored. Simple just means clear, even *obvious* once you discover it.

Through the course of this book, we are going to look at five STEPS we have found essential for helping us grow as fully devoted followers of Jesus Christ. These steps, developed over years of trial and error in our parish, take us in the direction of conforming our character, to become more like Jesus.

The five STEPS are *not* a checklist. Unfortunately, among churchgoers in general and Catholics in particular, it can be very easy to fall into a "check the box" mentality. We have been guilty of that ourselves. Go to Mass to fulfill your "obligation." Pray so that you can say you did. Do good and avoid evil to win God's favor or avoid his wrath. That is *not* what we are talking about.

We call them steps for three reasons. First of all, what we are proposing is a *journey*. As we noted yesterday, Jesus's original disciples were called "followers of the Way." Jesus introduced a new path forward for humanity that was radically different from anything history had witnessed before. Following Jesus means moving step by step down that path; it's a pilgrimage, and every step takes us forward. Second, we call them steps because as we take steps on a staircase, we achieve a higher level; we ascend to the place we want to go. Finally, we call them steps because, in all honesty, it makes for a great acronym, as we'll see.

Each step builds on a different aspect of our Catholic faith and can be repeated over and over again. We can practice them our whole life long. Think of them like the diet and exercise we might undertake in the interest of health and wellness. Exercise and endurance, cardio and carbs, and fruits and vegetables all form elements of a fitness regime. The same is true for these steps. Take one out, and you could limit your spiritual fitness.

Not all the steps will appeal to you in the same way. Some will fire you up and powerfully impact your faith. Others will be a greater challenge for you, and that's okay. The five STEPS both build your personal faith *and* build up the corporate Body of the Church. Jesus wants to grow and strengthen your personal relationship with him, and he wants to do the same for his community of believers. These two goals go hand in hand.

One other thing: they come in no particular order. You can start anywhere, wherever you want.

So, what, precisely, are the STEPS?

"S" Is for "Serve"

To follow Jesus means to serve others and develop a servant's heart. We can serve in our family, in our church family, and also further afield. Jesus came to serve. If we follow him, we will do the same.

"T" Is for "Tithe and Give"

We can tell you from personal experience and from the testimony of many parishioners that God became real for us when we started *giving*. And that's because giving reflects the character of God.

"E" Is for "Engage in Christian Community"

Jesus built a *community* of followers who formed a relationship with him *and* one another. We need friends in faith if we are to become more like Jesus.

"P" Is for "Practice Prayer and Sacraments"

We say *practice* prayer because it is something we have to do repeatedly. It takes practice to improve in prayer and to connect with God in the sacraments. Even the Eucharist, the source and summit of our faith life, requires practice to truly appreciate. We also say practice because our prayer and sacramental life were never meant to live in isolation from our day-to-day life. We put into practice what we discover in prayer.

"S" Is for "Share Your Faith"

Specifically, we mean sharing your faith with people who do not have faith or have lost hold of it. Along with tithing, this might be the most challenging of the STEPS for Catholics. Having a heart for people who do not know Jesus and helping them to connect to Jesus can really grow our faith.

Over the rest of our journey together we will explore each of these STEPS and how they can renew and revitalize your faith. So let's begin, one step at a time.

Reflect

Do you agree that following Jesus is simple but not easy? Why or why not?

Rank in order which of the STEPS interest you most.

What STEPS are present in your life right now? Which would be the most challenging step for you?

Rebuild

God, our heavenly Father,
thank you for the clear instruction your Son, Jesus, gave
so that I might grow in my love for you and others.
May I honor you today by loving the people around me.
In Jesus's name.
Amen.

Hear O Israel! The Lᴏʀᴅ is our God,
the Lᴏʀᴅ alone!
Therefore, you shall love the Lᴏʀᴅ, your God,
with your whole heart, and with your whole
being, and with your whole strength.

—Deuteronomy 6:4–5

WEEK TWO

Serve

DAY 8

Get Great

The world offers you comfort, but you were not
made for comfort. You were made for greatness.

—*Pope Benedict XVI*

Read

The first of our five STEPS is *serve*. The word *serve* refers to the performance of tasks or duties usually for another or others. You don't choose whether or not you serve. You *will* invest your time, talent, and energy somewhere because everyone serves *something* or *someone*.

Of course, we can be tempted to serve only ourselves. Lots of people do. We can arrange our lives around our comfort, convenience, pleasure, possessions, or power. As we've seen, the apostles began following Jesus for very self-serving reasons. They thought one day Jesus would be king of Israel and they would be large and in charge by association. Their aim was political power and worldly weight so that others would serve *them*.

The same is always and everywhere true throughout history. People get into politics or aspire to leadership of organizations to advance themselves and their agenda. Season after season, we are treated to fresh examples of greed in the financial community, corruption in politics, and self-serving corporate cultures. And it isn't just a problem found in Washington or Wall Street. Little fiefdoms can develop anywhere, from your homeowner's association to the PTA at your kid's school and even your local parish.

Tom: As Mel Brooks says in *History of the World*, "It's good to be the king." It feeds our ego when others have to defer to us because of our position. It inflates our sense of self-worth to go first or have the seat of honor. As the number two guy at a large parish, I know people pay a little extra attention when I speak, are sure to laugh when I tell a joke, and notice when I come into the room. I get thanked for work I didn't even do.

Today, many people aim for positions of leadership and influence with a professed purpose of serving others only to veil their true selfish intentions. In the ancient world, there was no such veil. No one wanted positions of power and authority to serve others; they wanted to be served, and they made no secret of it. That was the way of the world, and the apostles wanted in on it. So twice in Mark's gospel, Jesus teaches them about true greatness.

Greatness is a favorite topic for most people. We debate constantly, ceaselessly about it. Who was the greatest rock band of all time? The greatest third baseman? The greatest movie?

Tom: Led Zeppelin and Mike Schmidt.

Father Michael: And, just for the record, *The Godfather*, hands down.

The greatest players, performers, politicians, and powerbrokers are determined by the points they make, the awards they receive, the votes they win, and the dollars they amass. Greatness is based on merit. But that's *not* how God determines greatness. Jesus tells us there is another way: "Then he sat down, called the Twelve, and said to them, 'If anyone wishes to be first, he shall be the last of all and the servant of all'" (Mark 9:35). Entirely straightforward. Serving God and his purposes, especially by serving one another, is how we become great in God's eyes.

Next, Jesus gives the apostles an object lesson on what it means to be a "servant of all" (and when he says *all*, he means *all*): "Taking a child he placed it in their midst, and putting his arms around it he said to them, 'Whoever receives one child such as this in my name, receives me; and whoever receives me, receives not me but the One who sent me'" (Mark 9:36–37).

In our contemporary culture, which rightly values and celebrates children, it can be easy to miss what an original, and radical, approach this really was. In the ancient world, children were very low when it came to the social order, and female children lowest of all. In Latin, the word for child, *infans,* means "not speaking," as in, not welcome to speak. The view was simply that children brought no value to the household. Jesus taught the apostles to extend their service primarily to those who can do nothing for them. Serve the person who can't pay you back, who won't be able to make any kind of return on your investment, who really isn't able to do anything for you at all.

Even though Jesus slowed down and took great pains to teach this lesson that was so fundamental to being his friend and follower, the apostles apparently didn't get it. We know because just one chapter later he needs to make the same point all over again. Interestingly, it comes in the context of an alternatingly alarming and amazing forecast regarding his coming death and resurrection. Hearing such astounding predictions for future events would likely evoke wonderment or, on the other hand, disbelief. But neither seems to have been the case for these somewhat obtuse men. Instead, their thoughts were elsewhere: "Then James and John, the sons of Zebedee, came to him and said to him, . . . 'Grant that in your glory we may sit one at your right and the other at your left'" (Mark 10:35, 37).

The two brothers are seeking to secure for themselves the top posts in the Messiah's future government that they were dreaming about. With reliable patience in the face of their selfish and superficial request, Jesus responds: "You do not know what you are asking. Can you drink the cup that I drink or be baptized with the baptism with which I am baptized?" (Mark 10:38).

The "cup" is a metaphor in scripture for God's providential will, what he intends for someone. Sometimes the cup means a measure of blessing, but other times it suggests some form of suffering that must take place before the blessing can be poured out. Knowing that he will have to suffer in order to bring blessing to the world, Jesus understands the disciples will too if they want to be a part of his work: "They said to him, 'We can.' Jesus said to them, 'The cup that I drink, you will drink, and with the baptism with which I am baptized, you will be baptized; but to sit at my right or at my left is not mine to give but is for those for whom it has been prepared'" (Mark 10:39–40).

They will suffer for their service; Jesus can promise them that. But the positions of power and authority were, apparently, not his to give, belonging instead to his heavenly Father. But he takes this opportunity to repeat the point he previously made, only this time, he seems to go further: "Whoever wishes to be great among you will be your servant; whoever wishes to be first among you will be the slave of all" (Mark 10:43–44).

The greatest won't be just the *servant* of all, they will be the *slave* of all. Quite an assertion to make, but one that came in the context of his own even more remarkable sacrifice: "For the Son of Man did not come to be served but to serve and to give his life as a ransom for many" (Mark 10:45).

Above all people who ever lived, Jesus, as the Son of God, deserved to be served. But instead he came to serve. He emptied himself so that he could pour into other people. In response, on numerous occasions, the crowds were so astonished by his teaching and amazed by his miracles that they wanted to make him king. Jesus steadfastly resisted their efforts. He didn't accept that title until his Passion and Death, his greatest acts of service. As he laid down his life, his Roman persecutors, in one of the greatest ironies of history, posted above his head a simple sign, stating, "Jesus the Nazorean, the King of the Jews" (John 19:19). He was pronounced king not on a throne but on the Cross, crowned not with jewels but with thorns.

In your baptism, you were anointed with oil and named a "priest, prophet, and king." It is a kingship that must follow Jesus's own path of selfless service. That's the path to greatness.

Reflect

Whom do you admire because they use their influence or position in service to others?

As you look at your day-to-day life, who are the people you have an opportunity to serve? How can you serve them?

Rank on a scale of one to five how well you serve and add value to others. Why do you give yourself this number?

Rebuild

God, our heavenly Father,
through your Son's life and death on the Cross,
you have taught us that the path to greatness
comes through service.
In the course of this week, allow me to grow
to be more like your Son,
who came not to be served but to serve.
I pray through Christ our Lord.
Amen.

Whoever wishes to be first among you
will be the slave of all.

—Mark 10:44

DAY 9

But Go for the Mundane

Do small things with great love.
—*St. Teresa of Calcutta*

Read

We serve to become more like Jesus, who came not to be served but to serve and give his life for us. Growing our character to reflect Jesus means serving in what John Ortberg, in his book *The Life You've Always Wanted*, has called the "ministry of the mundane."

The ministry of the mundane means serving anywhere we see a need. Sometimes, rather than hoping someone else will do it, it's up to us to do the dishes, take out the trash, change a diaper, drive a kid to practice, clean an elderly friend's gutter, or listen with empathy to a neighbor in need. It's about doing the obvious thing everyone knows needs to be done but no one wants to do.

Jesus models this for us on the night before he died. The gospel writer John tells us, "Before the feast of Passover, Jesus knew that his hour had come to pass from this world to the Father. He loved his own in the world and he loved them to the end" (John 13:1). The "hour" in John's gospel always refers to Jesus's Passion. There was an appointed time for the crucifixion, and Jesus recognized it when it arrived. While on the surface it seemed his arrest and execution were imposed on him, John's gospel underscores that Jesus freely and deliberately chose the timing of those events. And he chose them motivated only by love.

The next verses tell us *why* Jesus could serve others out of selfless love: "So, during supper, fully aware that the Father had put everything into his power and that he had come from God and was returning to God, he rose from supper and took off his outer garments" (John 13:2–4). Jesus served others in the knowledge of who he was. *He knew he had come from God and was returning to God.* A servant's heart is formed in the deep knowledge of *who* we are and *whose* we are.

Jesus had the mission to save the world, but it did not stop him from a simple, humbling task that was about as mundane as you could get: "Then he poured water into a basin and began to wash the disciples' feet and dry them with the towel around his waist" (John 13:5).

The washing of feet in that time and place was an essential daily task. Because of the climate, people typically walked the streets with open-toed sandals. Dusty, unpaved roads, often littered with trash and excrement, made foot washing a must when arriving home. For guests, too, it was a necessity but also a form of greeting and an expression of hospitality.

Necessary and essential as it was, however, foot washing was relegated to the lowest of servants, usually female slaves. So it is easy to imagine the apostles' confusion when Jesus takes on the task that needed to be done that no one wanted to do. Jesus serves in both a *real* and a *symbolic* way. Real in that he actually washed the disciples' feet. He tied a towel around his waist, got down on his knees, and started washing feet: twelve guys, twenty-four feet. Even if he worked quickly, the job would easily have taken thirty to forty minutes. This was no publicity stunt done for a photo op. As far as we know, no one even saw him do it, besides the apostles themselves. Of course, it was *also* symbolic. Jesus was making a point, one that no one at table that evening would ever forget.

As with probably anyone in their position, the apostles would have been shocked and surprised by this shocking and surprising episode. Washing another's feet was beneath *their* dignity, much less that of their *rabbi*. The apostles, who, by this point, had already and often been amazed by Jesus, were probably astonished. Peter, as usual, is the first to speak up. He announces to Jesus, somewhat self-righteously, "You will never wash my feet" (John 13:8).

Though motivated by love and affection, Peter is putting his pride on display, even as Jesus is modeling profound humility. Sometimes we exhibit pride by refusing to serve and sometimes by not allowing others to serve us. We grow to be like Christ by *serving* but also, at times, being served. Previously, at Bethany, Jesus had allowed a woman to wash his feet (John 12:3). Christian community, like any healthy family, is marked by a culture of serving others and being served. We need both. Jesus helps Peter, and the other apostles, see that: "So when he had washed their feet [and] put his garments back on and reclined at table again, he said to them, 'Do you realize what I have done for you? You call me "teacher" and "master," and rightly so, for indeed I am. If I, therefore, the master and teacher, have washed your feet, you ought to wash one another's feet. I have given you a model to follow, so that as I have done for you, you should also do'" (John 13:12–15). Jesus powerfully reveals that no act of service is beneath him. And so, if we truly want to follow him, that means no act of service is beneath us.

Think about it: When we say something is beneath us, we're actually putting ourselves above Jesus. Often, we don't come right out and say it in so many words; that would sound too arrogant. The phrase we both find ourselves using far too often is maybe one that you use too. We say, "I shouldn't have to do this." There is a problem with an employee, and we say, "I shouldn't have to have this conversation." Some chore at home remains undone, and we think, *I shouldn't have to do* this *again*. That needy neighbor needs us, and we complain, "I shouldn't have to be bothered, I've got other things to do, *better* things to do!" That's setting a standard for ourselves that is different from the one Jesus challenges us to accept and demonstrated *how* to accept. And in demonstrating his standard, Jesus removes any ability on our part to make such excuses, summing it up, "Amen, amen, I say to you, no slave is greater than his master nor any messenger greater than the one who sent him" (John 13:16).

"Amen, amen." In other words, this is important, this is crucial, this is fundamental to rebuilding your Catholic faith. But it's important for another reason too. Jesus concluded: "If you understand this, blessed are you if you do it" (John 13:17).

At one level, the apostles clearly understood what Jesus had just done for them. It was so concrete, so unexpected, so profoundly dramatic, that they could hardly fail to recognize that it was a powerful lesson. But Jesus says that true understanding comes from *following* his example. We only know *and* understand the lessons that we put into practice. The ministry of the mundane, as with all the steps of discipleship, only pays off when we undertake it.

Reflect

What obstacles keep you from embracing a servant's heart?

What are the mundane tasks around you that no one else wants to do that you can do?

Who is an example of someone you know who does not mind serving in mundane ways? How do you think they grew into such maturity?

Rebuild

God, our heavenly Father,
thank you for your Son, Jesus, who was not afraid
to partake in the ministry of the mundane.
May I always understand that no task is beneath me,
remembering that I find my beginning and end in you.
Give me the eyes to see and the ears to hear
all the simple opportunities I have to serve others.
In Jesus's name.
Amen.

[Jesus said,] "I have given you a model to
follow, so that as I have done for you, you
should also do."

—John 13:15

DAY 10

Roll Away the Stone

*Charity is greater than any rule. Moreover, all
rules must lead to charity.*

—*St. Vincent de Paul*

Read

If you want to be great, you've got to serve. Serving is essential
to membership in nearly anything: a family, a team, a class, or a
staff. Belonging and serving go together.

Service is an everyday part of everyday life. And yet, some-
how, somewhere, this basic fact got lost sight of in the culture of
many Catholic parishes. Perhaps with the emphasis on "duty"
and "obligation," many Catholics approach church merely as a
consumer exchange. Their contribution is just showing up; after
that, they're expecting to be served.

Not only is this not helpful for the life of the parish, it's also
not healthy for the parishioners themselves. Why? Jesus said, "I
will build my church, and the gates of the netherworld shall not
prevail against it" (Matthew 16:18). When you start serving in
your parish, you are at work with Jesus building his Church. Discipleship requires getting up out of the pew and serving in some
specific way. However modest your role, however humble your
contribution, your service can be a part of his great big plan to
build the Church. Just as you grow closer to someone when you
work on a project together, whether it is tending a garden, com-
pleting a puzzle, or cooking a meal, when you join Jesus in the
project of building his Church, you will grow closer to him.

Also, serving in parish ministry is utterly different than serving your family, volunteering at your kid's school, or helping out at a local soup kitchen. The Church is Christ's Body. It is the visible presence of Christ to the world. When you choose to serve the Church, you are making Christ's presence more visible in your community.

How are we to serve? What are we to do? In Ephesians, St. Paul lists gifts and roles in the Church: "And he gave some as apostles, others as prophets, others as evangelists, others as pastors and teachers, to equip the holy ones for the work of ministry, for building up the body of Christ" (Ephesians 4:11–12).

The apostles, Jesus's closest friends and followers, helped form and grow the earliest life of the Church. Their successors today are the Order of Bishops. Prophets help the Church see what God is doing at any particular time as well as what he is going to do next. Evangelists have a gift for reaching people who haven't heard the Gospel. Then there are pastors and teachers who lead and instruct specific local Christian communities.

Obviously, very few are called to serve in those offices. But all of us are members of what Paul calls the "holy ones" to whom belongs the work of "ministry." What does that entail? Well, basically, everything that doesn't fall to the bishops, prophets, evangelists, pastors, and teachers.

The primary service of pastors and teachers, or church staff in a parish, is *not* to do the work of ministry for the parish. Rather, they are charged to equip members of the parish community to do ministry. You might want to read that again because, in most parishes, this is a novel idea. Unfortunately, there are many pastors and church staff members who forget this truth or simply don't even accept it. They want to serve the people themselves, so everything from greeting at the front door to handing out the bulletins after Mass is done by the pastor and perhaps his small circle of church people. However, the very best way for a pastor to serve his parishioners is to get *them* serving. As parish leaders, we rely on a very focused formula to do that. We call it *inspire, encourage, and equip.*

- **Inspire:** It's our job to paint a vision for the impact parishioners can have by serving in ministry.

- **Encourage:** We encourage the people in the pews to carve out time to serve and then thank them for doing it.

- **Equip:** We give volunteer ministers the tools they need to serve others well. This means a clear job description, training, and any resources necessary to serve effectively. It also means providing them with support when things don't go well. To properly equip them is to set them up for success.

Paul says it is up to church leaders to prepare people to serve in ministry. Then he continues reflecting on the impact serving has on the Church, as we build up the Body "until we all attain to the unity of faith and knowledge of the Son of God, to mature manhood, to the extent of the full stature of Christ" (Ephesians 4:13). That's a lot in one verse. Paul lists three outcomes when it comes to serving in the Church:

1. **Building Unity of Faith:** Parish communities that are divided have stopped working on common goals. When we serve with other Christ followers, we become more unified, forming connections with them. If you are someone who hates to see infighting and loves to promote mutual cooperation and teamwork, then serving in the parish is a great way to build a bond of unity.

2. **Growing in Knowledge of the Lord:** Every time we serve in our parish so that another will connect to Jesus Christ, *we* develop greater intimacy with him.

3. **Developing Maturity:** We "grow up" when we serve. Putting aside some of the time we would spend on ourselves and our own pleasures and pursuits and giving it away to serve God and his people develops maturity. It makes us a little less self-centered. Think about it: the only people who don't serve

or undertake chores in a family household are the babies. Every other member is usually expected to do something.

Serving helps us grow; it also helps the Church grow. It attracts other people to our parish because it simply makes the Church a more attractive environment.

This leads us to the story of a dead man. Well, actually the story of the dead man's friends. The raising of Lazarus from the dead represents one of Jesus's most spectacular miracles. Perhaps you know the story. Lazarus was a close friend of Jesus, so his sisters reach out to him on their brother's demise. When he comes to the tomb, there is, according to custom, a crowd of mourners. To them, collectively, he commands, "Take away the stone" (John 11:39).

This is a reference to the large stone covering the entrance to the tomb. After the mourners roll away the stone, Jesus says a quick prayer and then dramatically cries out in a loud voice, "Lazarus, come out!" (John 11:43).

And at that, Lazarus emerges from the tomb. Jesus raises Lazarus from the dead. He does the *impossible*. But he doesn't do the *possible*. He waits for the others to do what they can do on their own: rolling away the stone. Only after this simple task is complete does Jesus perform the miracle.

Father Michael: Simple service at your parish can roll away the stones, removing the obstacles that keep people from an encounter with Jesus Christ. Our small acts of hospitality can have a great big impact. For example, at our parish, our parking ministers help relieve the frustration of finding a parking spot, which can be *very* frustrating, especially if you have a car full of kids or are running late. A smile and a friendly word from our greeters at the door can answer a visitor's number one

question: "Am I welcome here?" Simple acts
of service in the parish remove real obstacles
from people coming to Christ.

In serving in ministry in our parish, we do the *possible*. And when we do, we get a front-row view of Jesus doing the *impossible*. We can see hearts healed, minds changed, and lives rebuilt. We experience God's glory and things we never thought possible. There will be times when we say, "That wasn't me, that was God working through me." However, if we never do the possible tasks in our parish, the simple things, we will never see these miracles; we will miss out on what God is doing.

Therefore what?

Serve your parish in a way that is of practical help; take a job that needs to be done, or that no one else wants to do. Most parishes don't have any trouble finding people who want to serve in high-profile roles as lectors, cantors, and, of course, the prestigious role aptly named "Extraordinary Ministers of the Eucharist." Neither is there usually a shortage of people who enjoy the platform for their views and opinions that the parish council provides. Don't start there.

Instead, as we saw yesterday, embrace the ministry of the mundane. We have seen many volunteer ministers in our parish who do things that would appear to be "beneath" them. There is the orthopedic surgeon who directs traffic in our parking lot. There is the multimillionaire investor who serves coffee in our café. There is a highly successful business owner who cleans our bathrooms between Masses. Despite their success in the world and their distinguished status, they choose to serve God and their parish in mighty mundane ways. We don't know much about your parish, but we can bet they are always looking for volunteer ministers. Such volunteers can be the lifeblood of any parish. Whether you feel completely disconnected from Jesus or have found yourself closer to him through the last ten days, you need to serve, and the parish needs your service. It is a match made in heaven.

Reflect

How do you think serving in your parish will draw you closer to Christ?

Why does Paul connect serving and spiritual maturity?

What opportunities do you see for volunteering in your parish?

Rebuild

God, our heavenly Father,
you have made me for ministry
and to serve the Church through my parish.
May my service bring unity to our community,
help me grow in knowledge of your Son,
and develop maturity in my faith.
Through our Lord Jesus Christ, your Son,
who lives and reigns with you in the unity of the Holy Spirit,
one God, forever and ever.
Amen.

And he gave some as apostles, others as prophets, others as evangelists, others as pastors and teachers, to equip the holy ones for the work of ministry, for building up the body of Christ.

—Ephesians 4:11–12

DAY 11

Serve Those in Need

Charity is that with which no man is lost, and
without which no man is saved.

—*St. Robert Bellarmine*

Read

Growing to become like Jesus means we look to serve those in
need. And there is no shortage of needy people, who can be *very*
needy in very many ways.

Some people require help because of traumatic life events.
We see the extreme cases of earthquakes, hurricanes, and other
natural disasters. More often, people find themselves needy due
to the loss of a loved one or a financial or health crisis. Others
need help because of the environment in which they live: think
of people in communities without access to clean water or neigh-
borhoods plagued by violence. Many find themselves in need
because of their own poor choices. And then, of course, there is
the convergence of crisis: environmental, situational, and generational calamities that leave people in crisis.

When it comes to serving those in need, we don't check our
brains at the door. Digging in to serve is critical. But, stopping to
reflect and examine what leads to the conditions you're addressing shows another level of concern for people. How you approach
the needs of others may reflect your personality too.

Father Michael: Our good friends Brian and Lisa invest generously in helping those in material need. Brian is a strategist, and so he gives his time to help service organizations become more effective and efficient. Lisa has a compassionate heart and loves helping people directly, one on one. Whether we are thinkers or feelers, we need to think through how our acts of charity impact others *and* actually act in charity.

Whatever our personality and whatever the reason people find themselves in need, we cannot escape Jesus's clear instruction to love the unloved and serve the unserved. Among other places, we find this direction in the twenty-fifth chapter of the Gospel of Matthew: "When the Son of Man comes in his glory, and all the angels with him, he will sit upon his glorious throne, and all the nations will be assembled before him. And he will separate them one from another, as a shepherd separates the sheep from the goats" (Matthew 25:31–32).

The passage is called the "Judgment of the Nations" because it looks to the end of time, when Jesus comes back as king to judge the living and the dead. All people, Christians and non-Christians alike, will be held accountable to the same standard. And that standard is basically all about addressing human need. An individual's record of service will determine their placement in one of two groups. To the first group he will say, "For I was hungry and you gave me food, I was thirsty and you gave me drink, a stranger and you welcomed me, naked and you clothed me, ill and you cared for me, in prison and you visited me" (Matthew 25:35–36).

Jesus gives us a clear and simple list of ways to serve people. We call these the "corporal works of mercy," the charitable actions by which we help our neighbors in their most basic physical needs. The message is that we have abundant opportunities to care for them if we will simply pay attention.

The passage continues, "Then the righteous will answer him and say, 'Lord, when did we see you hungry and feed you, or thirsty and give you drink? When did we see you a stranger and welcome you, or naked and clothe you? When did we see you ill or in prison, and visit you?' And the king will say to them in reply, 'Amen, I say to you, whatever you did for one of these least brothers of mine, you did for me'" (Matthew 25:37–40).

Reading the whole chapter, this list is repeated four times. Repetitive perhaps, but the repetition powerfully makes Jesus's intentions unequivocally clear. Such work needs to become an absolute priority for us because it has eternal consequences. The passage goes on to say that Jesus, the just judge, will condemn in the harshest possible language those who did not serve the needy, those who are in the second group. Their failure to serve "one of the least of these brothers of mine" is tantamount to refusing to serve him.

Wow!

Will Rogers once said, "It isn't the parts of the Bible I don't understand that bother me. It's the parts I *do*." Some people find this teaching challenging (that would include us); others, inspiring.

> **Tom:** Just recently I was talking to my friend Dave who works as a physician's assistant. He updated me on a career change. With great excitement he shared how he moved from working in the emergency room of a large suburban hospital to caring for the medical and physical needs of homeless and displaced people on city streets. He continued to get more animated as he spoke, gradually growing the most excited when he said, "And we even get to wash people's feet. How

> awesome is that? I get to wash people's feet, just like Jesus." Part of me loved witnessing his enthusiasm, and I was humbled by his heart. The other part of me thought, *I can't possibly see myself getting that excited about washing someone's feet.* I have a long way to go when it comes to serving others, especially people in need.

You may be like Dave and get excited at the thought of helping others in need. It might be the thing that fires you up about Jesus and makes you want to know him better. Or, conversely, serving in this way may push you out of your comfort zone. In either case, serving the needy is a key way to grow in your faith, and you won't know how serving will grow your faith until you try it.

Here are three suggestions when it comes to this kind of service:

1. Start looking. If you live in an urban area, the needy are probably in plain view, easy to identify. But guess what? They're present in suburban and rural communities too. In what way can *you* serve them, even if it is only saying hello and treating them with human dignity? If you can't think of someone in need, reread Matthew 25:35–36. Ask God for eyes to see who the people are whom you can serve right now.

2. Look for opportunities to serve together with your parish community. Just about every parish we know serves people in need in some way. Many have relationships with organizations that are feeding the hungry, helping the homeless, hosting food pantries, or serving mothers and children in crisis pregnancies. Check in with your parish to see what they are already doing. These opportunities may not be well advertised, but they are probably happening.

3. Consider going on a mission or service trip. This is definitely the deep end of the pool, but some people actually find it easier to block off a large chunk of time on their calendar rather than squeeze service into their weekly schedule. Your parish may or may not have such opportunities, but there are plenty of other churches and organizations that do. We have seen many people in our parish get turned on and worked up about their faith after going to a different part of our country or another place in the world and serving the disadvantaged.

In serving people with material needs, we grow in so many ways:

- We grow in understanding of our common humanity and the real needs around us.

- We grow in recognition that money and possessions do not bring happiness as we often experience the joy and gratitude of those in need.

- We grow in awareness of our own need for more joy and greater gratitude.

A reporter from the US spent a whole day observing Mother Teresa ministering "to the poorest of the poor" of Calcutta. At the end of the day, he said to her, "I would not do what you do for a million dollars." She kindly, but firmly, replied, "Neither would I." Christian service is about more than proper care of another's needs. It is about recognizing the image of God in others through our service. It is about allowing our service to open our eyes to God himself and fall more deeply in love with him. And you can't put a price on that.

Reflect

Does serving people in need because of faith in Jesus inspire you, or do you find serving others to be more challenging?

Are you more inclined to serve people directly or eliminate the larger issues that cause poverty? Why is it important to keep both approaches in mind when serving people in need?

What are the opportunities around you to serve those in need right now?

Rebuild

God, our heavenly Father,
thank you for this clear teaching of your Son.
Give me eyes to see the opportunities
you have put before me to meet the basic needs of others.
May the Holy Spirit give me the conviction and courage
to act on their behalf when I see those opportunities.
Through Christ our Lord.
Amen.

And the king will say to them in reply, "Amen, I say to you, whatever you did for one of these least brothers of mine, you did for me."

—Matthew 25:40

DAY 12

Determine Your Holy Discontent

> God has created us for some definite service. He
> has committed some work to me which he has not
> committed to another. I have my mission. . . . I am
> a link in a chain, a bond of connection between
> persons. He has not created me for naught. I shall
> do good. I shall do his work.
>
> —*St. John Henry Newman*

Read

Your life is not your project alone.

It is God's project as well. He had you in mind from all eternity and, at just the right time, formed you in your mother's womb, beginning the lifelong process of shaping you into exactly the person he wants you to be.

The world tells us to form our own dreams and fulfill our own desires. That's not terrible advice, but it's an approach that brings a lot of pressure. If we are not always sure what we should be doing or what we should be doing *next*—and most people seldom are—we can experience fear and anxiety.

But your life is not your project alone. It is a partnership with God. You are his work of art. However, unlike inanimate art or architecture, God invites your participation through the mission he has selected for you to do. St. Paul tells us in Ephesians 2:10

that there are good works he has created for you. God has a vision for good work only you can do based on who he has shaped you to be. The point is that your good works are not incidental to who you are. They are not something you do in addition to living your life. They flow out of who God has created you to be in Christ Jesus.

The question becomes, how do you *find* the work that God has given to you? Dozens of stories in scripture illustrate the point, but Moses's story is one of our favorites. Moses is a hero, for sure, but he's not a superhero. He's a very real man, every bit as fallible and flawed as we are. Through unexpected circumstances, Moses grew up in the royal court of the king of Egypt, the pharaoh. Though Jewish, he lived in luxury and privilege while the rest of his fellow Israelites lived in poverty and slavery. And, apparently, that bothered him to his core. One day, he saw a fellow Hebrew being beaten by an Egyptian taskmaster, and the scene so deeply disturbed him that he became consumed with murderous rage, killing the Egyptian. While his violence was dreadful, his discontent was of God and could be called holy.

As the story proceeds, his crime was discovered, and Moses was forced to flee the country. Settling in a foreign land, he goes on to begin a family, find a new career, and build a comfortable, quiet life for himself. All the while, the slavery of his own people weighed heavy on his heart, but he did nothing about it. It seemed there was nothing he *could* do, until . . .

One day, Moses was tending the flock of his father-in-law, Jethro. "Leading the flock beyond the wilderness, he came to the mountain of God, Horeb. There the angel of the LORD appeared to him as fire flaming out of a bush. When he looked, although the bush was on fire, it was not being consumed. So Moses decided, 'I must turn aside to look at this remarkable sight. Why does the bush not burn up?'" (Exodus 3:1–3).

Moses was living his very normal, somewhat boring, everyday routine. And suddenly, God puts a burning bush in his path.

A burning bush is actually quite common in the desert, but what is *not* common is that the bush was not consumed. God got Moses's attention, but he does not speak to Moses until Moses *turns aside*. In other words, he had to stop what he was doing, step away from the work he was undertaking that day, and start paying attention to what God was doing.

"The LORD said: I have witnessed the affliction of my people in Egypt . . . so I know well what they are suffering. Therefore, I have come down to rescue them from the power of the Egyptians and lead them up from that land into a good and spacious land" (Exodus 3:7–8). God wasn't watching from a distance. Instead, he saw the pain and problems of his people up close and in real time. He shared with Moses the good news that he had a vision for a better future for the Israelites. His plan included their release from slavery, escape from Egypt, and the taking possession of a new homeland of blessing and abundance. But that's not all . . .

"Now, go! I am sending you to Pharaoh to bring my people, the Israelites, out of Egypt" (Exodus 3:10). God says, "Good news! I have seen the suffering of my people and I am going to do something about it. I am going to lead them to a blessed and grace-filled place. Even better news, I am going to use *you*, Moses. You are my favored instrument and chosen leader."

Like Moses, you may observe pain and suffering in the world that hurts your heart: the forgotten homeless, the neglected hungry, the endangered unborn, or the abandoned elderly. Perhaps pervasive poverty, escalating incivility, or unceasing violence especially worry you. You see the problems of the world, and you find it disturbing; you can feel that holy anger or discontent that Moses felt.

Some problems just capture your attention more than they bother other people. That's okay. There are so many problems in the world that we can't care about all of them equally. However, as Christ followers, if we are to know the special mission God has for us, we have to pay attention to what bothers us most.

Then we must be prepared to say yes when God invites us to do something about it.

So Moses dreamt of an end to the Israelites' slavery. God wanted Moses to undertake the problem. Seems like a great match, so Moses was like "Send me in coach!" right? Well, not quite: "Moses said to God, 'Who am I that I should go to Pharaoh and bring the Israelites out of Egypt?'" (Exodus 3:11).

Moses immediately felt overwhelmed by the task. *Who am I to do such a thing? I'm just a shepherd, a nobody, in the middle of nowhere, an everyday kind of guy doing an everyday kind of job. Who am I to go to the most powerful man in the world and negotiate the release of his largely free labor force, upon which his whole country's economy is based?* It struck Moses as a crazy idea, doomed to failure and fraught with peril. How can *he* be expected to do anything about it?

You might feel that way when it comes to issues or concerns that are on your heart, whether they are worldwide problems, systemic problems, or generational problems. How can you be expected to do anything about them?

> **Tom:** The mission of my life is to make Catholic parishes relevant to their communities. I admit, that is fairly ambitious. But I will never forget when I was drawn into this mission. I was at a conference and one of the speakers used the phrase "irrelevant church environments." And in that moment it struck me, with complete clarity, that my heart breaks when I see the Catholic Church I love and serve drift into irrelevance in community after community. The problem is that people think we have nothing to offer, that we're out of touch with their day-to-day lives.
>
> Quite honestly, I still tear up when I think of those words. I knew my vocation was to

> devote my life to a local parish and help oth-
> ers do the same. But even while that call was
> so strong and I so clearly saw what God wanted
> from me, I questioned it for years, wondering
> if God could use such a flawed person.

Moses looks at his role as a shepherd and says, "I can't go to the pharaoh." But "God answered: I will be with you" (Exodus 3:12). God essentially says, "It's not about who *you* are, Moses; it's about who *I* am. I will be with you and because I have said I am leading the people out of Egypt; it will happen."

Of course, Moses immediately agrees, right? Who would argue with God? Well, arguing is exactly what Moses proceeded to do. He goes on to list four more excuses we'll be looking at tomorrow. He explains exactly why he cannot serve God and the mission he has for his life. *His* excuses are often *our* excuses.

Like Moses, we experience this strange dichotomy in ourselves. We want our lives to matter, yet we resist the very call to live out our purpose. We will look at that more tomorrow. For today, think about the problems that disrupt, even disturb, your heart, that seem to bother you more than others. Make a list, and then offer it up in prayer.

Reflect

What problems in the world bother you that you would like to solve?

Have you ever made excuses for not addressing issues you care deeply about? What are they?

What intimidates you about God calling you to serve?

Rebuild

God, our heavenly Father,
I believe you have created me for some good work
that is mine alone to do,
as it speaks to the deepest desires of my heart.
Help me to see where you have put a burning bush
in my life and give me the grace
to turn aside and pay attention.
I pray all these things through Christ, our Lord.
Amen.

For we are his handiwork, created in Christ Jesus for the good works that God has prepared in advance, that we should live in them.

—Ephesians 2:10

DAY 13

Make No Excuses;
Embrace the Mission

You will never be happy
if your happiness depends on getting solely what you want.
Change the focus. Get a new center.
Will what God wills, and your joy no man shall take from you.

—*Ven. Fulton Sheen*

Read

There is strong evidence to suggest that the happiest, most content, and most productive people—in fact, the most motivated people—don't approach their work as just a job or a paycheck. Neither do they see what they do as a path to greater privilege and position. Instead, they view their work as a calling, as a way in which they serve others and make a contribution to the world.

God has created you to serve him. And he calls you to serve in some very *specific* service. That service may be in addition to the work you *currently* do, or it might be the *next* thing you do or the work you *eventually* do. On the other hand, it could be a matter of learning to look at your current work through a different lens, recognizing how it already honors God and serves his purposes.

God calls us into his service, yet many people miss the call altogether because they're not paying attention. But even if we *are* paying attention, our tendency is to resist, to make excuses.

It's human nature. Even Moses himself made excuses. God called him to a powerful position, charged with leading the Israelites out of Egypt. It was to be a critical role in the history of the world and the whole story of salvation, "'But,' said Moses to God, 'If I go to the Israelites and say to them, "The God of your ancestors has sent me to you," and they ask, "What is his name?" what do I tell them?' God replied to Moses: I am who I am. Then he added: This is what you will tell the Israelites: I AM has sent me to you" (Exodus 3:13–14).

Moses tells God, "I don't really know you all that well. I don't even know your name, so how am I supposed to represent you?" God answers Moses's objection by *revealing* his name. In the Old Testament, a name reveals and reflects a person's character. In asking for his name, Moses is seeking understanding of God's nature and character. The name *Yahweh*, literally "I am" in Hebrew, underscores that God is preexistent and eternal, unchanging, wholly other than humanity and yet present to us.

He reveals his character to Moses as an initial contribution to the relationship. This, in turn, leads to a second objection or concern that Moses raises: "'But,' objected Moses, 'suppose they do not believe me or listen to me? For they may say, "The LORD did not appear to you"'" (Exodus 4:1). Of the five objections Moses raises, this one probably has the most merit. To accomplish his mission, Moses will have to convince the leaders of Israel that God wants *him* to lead them. And he immediately recognizes the challenge of credibility, given that he is an outsider and the proposed message is monumental and, frankly, unbelievable. However, "The LORD said to him: What's in your hand? 'A staff,' he answered. God said: Throw it on the ground. So, he threw it on the ground and it became a snake. . . . Then the LORD said to Moses, . . . That is so they will believe that the LORD . . . did appear to you" (Exodus 4:2–5).

God reassures Moses that he will, in fact, equip and empower him for the job. He can proceed with confidence that the Lord is with him to support and sustain him. This happens in our lives as well. When God calls us to serve him, the call often comes with signs of encouragement as well as the necessary ability to undertake the work. The call, signs, and ability are indications we are going in the right direction.

Even so, despite God dramatically revealing to Moses his presence and power, Moses continues to push back: "If you please, my Lord, I have never been eloquent, neither in the past nor now that you have spoken to your servant; but I am slow of speech and tongue" (Exodus 4:10). Of all Moses's objections, this is the most basic: he's simply not competent for the proposed mission. He can't speak well. In fact, he evidently suffered from a speech impediment, a legitimate obstacle for someone charged to be a spokesman and envoy.

> **Father Michael:** This lack of competency is the most common excuse I hear from parishioners when it comes to serving in mission or ministry at the parish: "I don't have the background," "I don't have the experience," "I don't know the Bible well enough," "I am not a church person," or even "I'm not 'holy' enough."

"The LORD said to him: Who gives one person speech? Who makes another mute or deaf, seeing or blind? Is it not I, the LORD? Now go, I will assist you in speaking and teach you what you are to say" (Exodus 4:11–12). The Lord explains to Moses that the very competencies he claims to lack are actually God-given gifts. In a subsequent verse, he goes on to indicate that when it comes to the public speaking part of the job, Moses's brother, Aaron, will help him out. That is an important point. When God calls us to serve or solve a problem, we are never alone. He wants to work with us, and he wants us to work with others to accomplish his mission.

So Moses raises all these objections, and one by one, God patiently answers them. God was patient, but Moses was frustrated, concluding, "If you please, my Lord, send someone else!" (Exodus 4:13). His final argument is no argument at all. Essentially, Moses tells God, "I'd rather not." And how does God respond to this objection? Well, he finally loses his patience: "The LORD became angry with Moses" (Exodus 4:14). Essentially, God just tells Moses, "You're going! Enough of the excuses; it's time to get to work." Of course, Moses ultimately cooperated, and as reluctant as he had been, we know from the rest of the story that he embraced his mission with passion and purpose. He becomes the very epitome of commitment and determination.

When we are *not* doing what God calls us to do, what we know we *should* do, there is a gnawing feeling in us that we are wasting our time, perhaps even our life. A sadness haunts our hearts; emptiness creeps into our souls. On the other hand, when we embrace the mission God has for us, our hearts and souls come alive. We have a reason for getting out of bed in the morning, energy and enthusiasm for living, and no trouble falling asleep at night.

> **Father Michael:** One of my favorite scenes from the movie *The Passion of the Christ* comes after Jesus's sentencing at the Roman Praetorium. Before he is led away in chains, the cross beam from which he will hang on Calvary is brought out and thrust upon him to carry. He doesn't so much lay hold of it as he hugs it lovingly. In that moment, Jesus embraces his mission.

We find our mission and purpose by discovering how God has created us and called us to love and serve him and others. God's call *will* align with our deepest desires, but that's only one aspect. God's call also aligns with our gifts *and*, surprisingly, our weaknesses, our personality, our experiences, and the unique problems of our generation. Accepting and following God's call in our life will take us to surprising places, and it can lead us home as it did for Moses.

> **Tom:** After a conversion experience in college, our good friend, Frank, left Baltimore and went to Japan to be a missionary, fairly sure that was God's mission for him. But there, much to his discomfort, he heard God calling him with a different plan: something about lacrosse and his parent's business. It didn't seem to add up, but it had his attention. Shortly thereafter, his father unexpectedly asked him to come home and help the family just for a year, and Frank knew it was a call from the Lord. Today, thirty-five years later, he's running a God-honoring company whose amazing success provides employment for hundreds of people as well as philanthropy in the community that benefits thousands of others. Meanwhile, he has been the vision-caster and prime mover in introducing the next generation to Christ through the Fellowship of Christian Athletes lacrosse program in his hometown, elsewhere in the country, and more recently, internationally. God's call sometimes brings us far away, and sometimes it takes us right back to familiar circumstances but with a new perspective.

> **Father Michael:** Our good friend Mike grew up in Chicago and from a very young age developed a great work ethic and an acumen for business. This combination along with solid values and a firm faith in God brought him success in retail at the national level. Throughout his career, however, he knew he wanted to

serve the Church in some solid and substan-
tive way. In retirement, that is exactly what he
is doing. Leveraging his leadership skills, he
has become a trusted and increasingly invaluable advisor at the parish and archdiocesan
level in a wide variety of projects from Catholic education to evangelization and parish
renewal. He has also demonstrated leadership in his financial support for the Church.

God has called you to do him some definite service. Perhaps
it's unclear right now what that is. Maybe you will not understand
it all in one flash of insight, but it can become clearer over time. It
begins by "turning aside" to see what God wants you to see, hearing his voice, and going where he wants you to go. God invites
you, whoever you are and whatever you've done, into mission to
serve his purposes. And he does so for one very simple reason: so
that you can come to know him better. We get to know and grow
in God through service. As we work on a common project and
fulfill the desires of our heart and God's heart, we become friends
and allies with God.

We see this so clearly in the life of Moses. In his initial encounter, Moses is so intimidated that he can't even look at God. Hid-
ing his face, he doesn't know how to address him or what to say
(Exodus 3:6). But, by the end of Moses's story, he talks to God
daily and easily, face-to-face, as if speaking to a friend (Exodus
33:11). What happened in between? They worked together on a
common project. Moses's service introduced him into a growing
relationship with the Lord, a relationship that became a friendship. That's how service works.

Reflect

How do you view your work and day-to-day responsibilities—
as a job, a career, or a calling?

What's on your heart? What and who is at hand to help?
What can you do today to pursue God's call on your life?

What excuses are you using to keep you from serving God
and pursuing his mission for your life?

Rebuild

God, our heavenly Father,
I give you thanks for the unique calling you have given me.
Help me to better understand the work
you have prepared for me and the role that only I can fill
in the coming kingdom of your Son.
In my service, may I come to know and love you more fully.
Through our Lord Jesus Christ, your Son,
who lives and reigns with you in the unity of the Holy Spirit,
one God forever and ever.
Amen.

[The LORD said to Moses:]
"Now go, I will assist you."

—Exodus 4:12

DAY 14

Develop a Servant's Heart

Thus should one regard us: as servants of Christ.

—*St. Paul*

Read

Throughout this section, we have looked at how service connects us to Jesus Christ in a unique way. When we invest our time and talent to serve God and others, we grow in true greatness, become more like Christ, contribute to the growth of God's kingdom, lift others up from their needs, and find our true calling and purpose in life. Best of all, we step into a growing friendship with God.

These are great blessings and high rewards that flow from serving. But for service to bear all this wonderful fruit in our lives, we must have the *right heart*.

Perhaps Jesus's most famous parable is called the parable of the prodigal son. The parable contrasts a younger brother, who leaves his home and family and recklessly squanders his inheritance, with an older, more responsible brother who stays home and dutifully does his duty. While much preaching and teaching focuses on the younger brother and his disobedience to the father, which most of the story concerns itself with, we want to take today's reflection to look at the older brother. After the younger brother returns home, and the father throws him a party, here's what happened: "[The older brother] became angry, and when he refused to enter the house, his father came out and pleaded with him. He said to his father in reply, 'Look, all these years I served you and not once did I disobey your orders; yet you never gave me even a young goat to feast on with my friends. But when your son returns who swallowed up your property with prostitutes, for him you slaughter the fattened calf'" (Luke 15:28–30).

The older son served the father faithfully. *But* he resented it. From his own words, and the tone they strike, it is clear he doesn't serve out of love. He serves purely out of obligation. Apparently, for years he has been quietly building up a case in his heart that his father *owes* him for his service. He considers the father in his debt, which is ironic because as the older son he would eventually inherit the entire estate. In serving the father, he himself would benefit, at least in the long term. But, instead, he was focused, in a mean-spirited, short-sighted kind of way, on the party the father was giving his brother.

The older son treats his father with resentment and disrespect, yet the father does not respond in kind. Just as the father treats the younger son with compassion and mercy in the face of his disregard and ingratitude, he treats the older brother in the same way. He says, "My son, you are here with me always; everything I have is yours" (Luke 15:31). All the father had was available to his son at any time. The older son had only to ask, and the father would have shared it with him. There was no reason for resentment.

Unexpectedly, when we start serving God, over time, we can come to resent it. Perhaps that is why you have never wanted to serve at church. You've seen people at your parish, and so have we, who have served for years, and they *aren't* happy or joyful about it. Instead, they're ungenerous, grumpy, and probably burnt out. This happens with priests and church staff as well. And it can be found in families all the time too: a sibling perhaps, who stays at home caring for aging parents, resenting the other siblings' lack of assistance.

Another common heart issue becomes feelings of entitlement. People serve in a role so long they begin to feel a misplaced sense of ownership, even privilege. At church, it is the lector who never prepares yet insists on reading at "his" Mass. It is the cantor who simply lacks the skill to lead people in worship and yet demands to hold the position and is, in fact, insulted at the mere suggestion of stepping down. But it isn't unique to parish life, as it is found in every sector. It's the small business owner who is just mailing it in because he can get away with it and shortchanging his customers in the process. It's the teacher who lets her students slide out of fatigue or boredom. And the list goes on and on.

Along with resentment and entitlement, we know we have gotten off track in our service when we serve to impress others, win favor, or simply look good. Our service ceases to be service when the focus is on anything other than honoring God.

When we lose our *why* we lose our *way*. When we forget that we serve to grow closer to Christ and become like him, our efforts, at best, become a chore. However, when we keep the purpose of loving God and loving others front and center, we keep the right *heart*.

> **Tom:** A few years ago, we undertook a capital campaign to build a new church building. It needed to be done, as our congregation was growing. But it was a daunting project in many ways, especially the challenge to raise millions of dollars.
>
> We interviewed consultants to advise us on fundraising, and I remember a conversation with one of them. He could see the fear in my eyes as I talked about the campaign. He said, "Tom, you know you don't *have* to do this; you *get* to do this." Those words changed my whole attitude toward the campaign. And while there were still many doubts and struggles ahead, I repeatedly kept coming back to his words.

You *get* to serve the Lord and his people. It is the privilege of a lifetime. If you hold a volunteer ministry position in your church, it is a privilege to serve as a lector, greeter, or parish council member. If you are a leader or manager of an organization, you have the opportunity to make decisions that influence and impact others. If you have been called to teaching or coaching, you enjoy the honor of forming and challenging young minds. If you are a parent, raising children is a blessing for you. If you earn a living for your family, you bear the responsibility to provide for them. You get to make a contribution to the lives and well-being of others.

Take one more look at the parable of the prodigal son. On an estate, such as the one suggested in the parable, there would be three levels of workers. In the first or lowest level were the outdoor laborers and the household staff. They did menial jobs that did not require much skill. In return for their labor, they received food, housing, protection from the owner of the estate, and, usually, a small stipend. Obviously, they had very limited options when it came to employment, and there was not much chance for upward mobility.

The second group of people were paid craftsmen. They possessed the basic skills needed for the operation of the estate. So not only would they receive room and board but also a salary, in some cases a handsome one, for their services.

The third group working on the estate were family members. They served the estate not simply because of what they were paid or what was provided for them through the estate but because it was their family business; it belonged to them. The connection ran much deeper than simple compensation. Their service was about who they were; it was about their *identity*.

We do not serve God as laborers or craftsmen but as sons and daughters. We work in the family business. It is a business we will inherit one day. Every act of service we perform, to love God and love others, builds more of our share of the estate we will receive in heaven.

God always has more blessings in store for us. He is always pouring blessings on us. And that's where we will go next in our STEPS.

Reflect

Considering today's challenge, what one action step do you need to take to stengthen your commitment to serving others?

In what ways do you need to guard your heart against poor attitudes about service?

After spending a week on the first of our STEPS, serve, why would you say it is a privilege to serve God and his purposes?

Rebuild

God, our heavenly Father,
help me to keep a humble heart as I serve others.
Protect me from an attitude of resentment,
entitlement, or ingratitude.
Grant me the grace to always remember the privilege
of serving you and others.
In Jesus's name.
Amen.

> With all vigilance guard your heart,
> for in it are the sources of life.
>
> —Proverbs 4:23

WEEK THREE

Tithe and Give

DAY 15

You Can't Outgive God

God will not be outdone in generosity.
—*St. Ignatius Loyola*

Read

Congratulations on making it this far and not being intimidated by the second of our STEPS: *tithe and give.*

The Church is accused of dwelling on money; it is often cited as a contributing factor for people walking away from organized religion. That perspective can distract us from what God has to say about the topic. We start this discussion not on dollars and cents but on the mystery of our faith.

The Catholic faith holds three chief mysteries. These are the core tenets of our faith that we cannot completely comprehend or understand but nonetheless are true. The first mystery states there is *one* God in *three* divine persons; this is the mystery of the Trinity. Think about that. God did not create the world out of boredom, or because he was looking for something to do. He wasn't lonely and in need of company and so created people for friendship and fellowship. In fact, God is a vibrant community of love, already perfect in and of himself. Purely out of his love, God created the world as an extension of his love and generosity.

God is generous. That's not a word we throw around lightly as it is often overused, but we can confidently describe our God as generous. Generous means showing a readiness to give more of something, freely giving or sharing. That's God.

Think of the generosity of God as expressed in Creation. He did not just make this world functional so that we could merely exist. God created a world of breathtaking beauty and endless splendor: stunning sunrises and sunsets, majestic mountains and verdant valleys. He created pristine beaches and deep blue oceans, starry nights and gently raining days. Scripture itself underscores the same point: "The heavens declare the glory of God" (Psalm 19:2). Creation tells of God's glory and his generosity, its greatness and grandeur overflowing out of his love for us.

God loves, so God gives.

But that's not even his greatest gift. In the Gospel of John we read, "For God so loved the world that he gave his only Son, so that everyone who believes in him might not perish but might have eternal life" (John 3:16).

The Incarnation, the gift of God's Son, is the *second* chief mystery of our faith. God is so generous that when we turned our back on him through sin, he *didn't* turn his back on us. Instead, he gave us his Son. And in the man Jesus we see the generosity of God on full display. He is generous in the wealth of his preaching and teaching. He gives freely by feeding the hungry, healing the sick, and raising the dead.

In his first miracle, Jesus turns water into wine so that a newlywed couple and their family would not be embarrassed and disappointed at their wedding party. Jesus does this when the party has been well underway, and yet he doesn't just make a modest amount of wine. Instead, he has six stone jars, each carrying twenty to thirty gallons of water, filled to the brim—in total 180 gallons, which would be over 900 bottles of wine. And he doesn't make cheap wine either; his was the choicest. Wine in scripture symbolizes abundance and joy. God gives this gift abundantly and joyfully.

In the miracle of the loaves and fish, Jesus takes five loaves and two fish and feeds five thousand people with this meager supply. The gospels tell us that after the crowd had been fed, he sent the apostles out to collect an abundance of leftovers (John 6:12–13). Sometimes God provides more than we need.

God loves, so God gives.

Behind these miracles and so many others, Jesus teaches about the generous heart of God, but it's all preparatory to the generosity Jesus would ultimately display. In his Passion, Jesus doesn't just provide help and healing, he shares *his very self.* Giving himself as the "Lamb of God" who takes away the sins of the world, he removed all barriers between us and God the Father.

Freely handing himself over to the Jewish leaders and Roman authorities, he allowed himself to be arrested and chained, mocked and humiliated, beaten and bloodied, and then nailed to the Cross. He willingly died a painful death out of love for us. He paid the debt we owe for our sin. And this total and complete sacrifice continues to be revealed and received each time we celebrate the Eucharist. At Mass, in Holy Communion, Jesus Christ again and again gives himself to us.

God loves, so God gives.

God gives us a new life through the power of the Resurrection, and this is the *third* chief mystery of our faith. Jesus rose from the dead; he conquered death once and for all and forever. And *because* he rose from the dead, we will too.

Finally, Jesus goes ahead of us to prepare a place for us in heaven. He prepares a place perfectly suited for how he created us, a place where we will forever know his goodness and live in community with others who know him and love him, a place of light and life.

God loves, so God gives.

God's heart is full of love and generosity toward us. Paul writes, "What then shall we say to this? If God is for us, who can be against us? He who did not spare his own Son but handed him over for us all, how will he not also give us everything else along with him?" (Romans 8:31–32). If God gave us his best when he gave us his Son, which he did, then it should come as no surprise that God gives to us with vast generosity in many other ways too. So when we look at how to use the gifts he has given to us, we are charged to reflect the nature and character of the giver.

We'll see through the course of this week that more than anything else, giving shows and grows our faith and trust in God. Our minds and hearts need to be renewed in understanding that we serve a generous and gracious God who wants to give us abundantly more than we can ask or imagine and invites us to provide for others.

God loves, so God gives. Same for us.

Reflect

Do you find it easy to believe that God is generous? Why or why not?

What gifts has God given you recently?

What do you have in abundance that you could share with others?

Rebuild

God, our heavenly Father,
I stand before your goodness and generosity.
May I grow to see that goodness and generosity in my life,
especially the gift of your Son's sacrifice on the Cross.
Help me to know your abundance.
Through your Son, Jesus.
Amen.

For God so loved the world that he
gave his only Son,
so that everyone who believes in him might
not perish but might have eternal life.

—John 3:16

DAY 16

Don't Worry (about Money)

Anxiety is the greatest evil that can befall a soul except sin. God
commands you to pray, but he forbids you to worry.

—*St. Francis de Sales*

Read

God loves us, so God gives to us. Just as any good father provides
for his children, it is in God's nature to provide for our needs.
Out of this truth we can then begin to comprehend what Jesus
teaches us about money and possessions in the twelfth chapter
of Luke's gospel. He said to his disciples, "Therefore I tell you, do
not worry about your life and what you will eat, or about your
body and what you will wear. For life is more than food and the
body more than clothing" (Luke 12:22–23).

The origin of the word *worry* is the verb "to choke." Worry
chokes the joy out of life. Jesus knows that human nature, always
and everywhere, has a tendency to worry; it probably goes back
to the origins of humanity and the instinct to survive.

First-century Christians worried about basic necessities.
They had to, as most lived their lives on the cusp of what would
look like deep poverty to us. Many people today still do. For
others of us, especially in suburban communities in first world
countries, that isn't our major concern. Some of us have plenty
of everything, yet we still worry about money. We worry if we'll
have enough to pay for our kids' education. We worry about
maintaining our standard of living and continuing to afford our

entertainment and recreational interests. We worry if we've saved enough for our retirement. We worry we'll outlive our money. Our culture is proof that there is no amount of money that can take away our worry for it.

Jesus says there is more to life than just meeting our needs. There is more to life than money. You may think, *I know that. I know that life is about relationships with God and others. I know life is about having purpose and meaning, forming a vision, and pursuing a mission. I know that life is about serving others. I know that life goes much deeper than physical needs . . . but . . .* We all know it intellectually, but at times that knowledge isn't enough to forestall worry corrupting our heart and robbing our joy.

Next Jesus asks a great question: "Can any of you by worrying add a moment to your life-span?" (Luke 12:25). Worrying about our money and possessions doesn't add any value to our life. In fact, there is plenty of medical evidence to suggest just the opposite. Worry and the stress it brings can prompt myriad physical and emotional problems that actually shorten the average lifespan. Besides, worrying is no fun. Have you ever looked back on time spent worrying with any sense of joy or accomplishment? No. None of us enjoy the experience, and it never makes a situation any better.

So why do we do it then? Jesus addresses that in the next verse: "If even the smallest things are beyond your control, why are you anxious about the rest?" (Luke 12:26). Worry, especially about money and possessions, often stems from thoughts about the future, a future that we don't and can't control. We worry about the economy. We worry about world events. We worry about space aliens. We worry because it gives us the false illusion of control. Accepting that much of life is *beyond* our control and believing it is never *outside* God's control is a better way to live. More successful living recognizes God is for you. God wants to provide for you.

Jesus returns to this point: "Notice how the flowers grow. They do not toil or spin. But I tell you, not even Solomon in all his splendor was dressed like one of them. If God so clothes the grass in the field that grows today and is thrown into the oven tomorrow, will he not much more provide for you, O you of little faith?" (Luke 12:27–28). As we have already noted, the beauty and splendor of nature is proof positive of the generosity and abundance of God. In the face of such beauty and splendor, our worry is actually a reflection of our lack of faith in God, perhaps even an affront to him. Worry is an outcome of faint or failing faith.

> **Tom:** In writing this section, I find it very convicting. As a father of eight, there's always a lot to worry about. I woke up early one recent morning worrying over a particularly challenging issue regarding family finances. Eventually, instead of just allowing my imagination to race through one worst-case scenario after another, I turned to prayer. There, I heard rather distinctly, "Tom, O you of little faith. Your faith in me is small right now and it needs to grow. *You* need to grow."

Next, Jesus gets to the root cause of our worry: "As for you, do not seek what you are to eat and what you are to drink, and do not worry anymore" (Luke 12:29).

Seek is an important word here. Jesus repeats it three more times in the next few verses. He says don't seek food and drink, as seeking those things leads to worry. What does that mean? Don't provide for yourself and your family? Avoid the grocery store? Hope your friends organize a meal train for you?

By *seek*, Jesus means setting your heart on what you're looking for. *Seek* means it becomes the all-consuming passion of your heart. Worry is not a *material needs* issue; it is a *heart* issue.

There are people with far more money and possessions than you who worry about money more than you. And there are people with far less money and possessions than you who worry about money and possessions less than you do.

Jesus continues, "All the nations of the world seek for these things, and your Father knows that you need them" (Luke 12:30). By "all the nations of the world," Jesus is referring to the Gentiles, the non-Jews who have not yet received the word of God. He means people who don't know that God is their Father and that it is in his nature to provide for his children. He means people who don't really believe in God and think that they are all alone in the world. When we worry about money and possessions, we act like practical atheists.

After answering the question of what *not* to do, Jesus tells us what *to* do when we worry about money. And, like most of Jesus's answers, it is incredibly simple and straightforward without beings simplistic. "Instead, seek his kingdom, and these other things will be given you besides" (Luke 12:31).

There's that word again: *seek*. Seek God and his kingdom. His kingdom refers to the places where his will is honored and served.

Where's that? It can be found anywhere, including in your own heart.

Every time we require provision, which is daily, and every time we even feel the gap between what we have and what we need, we have an opportunity to seek God, to draw closer to him and let more of his kingdom rule over our hearts. In those moments, we gratefully remember our rich inheritance as children of the most-high God and Father and renew our trust, which will build our trust, in his provision. That's why it is most important, and certainly not just a charming custom, to say a brief prayer of thanksgiving before meals.

Jesus concludes: "Do not be afraid any longer, little flock, for your Father is pleased to give you the kingdom" (Luke 12:32). Worry and fear are related. And they aren't just cousins; they're siblings. Don't be afraid, because God is pleased; it is his good pleasure to share with us his kingdom. It pleases God to provide us with what we *need* and even, when appropriate, what we *want*.

But his promise goes beyond that. When God provides for us, he wants to give us more than just the material need. He wants to meet the needs of our soul. He wants to establish his kingdom in our hearts. The kingdom is not *less* than our material needs; it is *more*. The kingdom is not aiming *lower*; it is aiming *higher*. As C. S. Lewis wrote in *Mere Christianity*, "Aim at Heaven and you will get earth 'thrown in': aim at earth and you will get neither."

Seek first his kingdom.

Reflect

On a scale of one to five, how much do you worry about money? (Five means you worry all the time and one means barely ever.) Why did you place yourself where you did on the scale?

What, specifically, are you worrying about currently? What do you worry about consistently?

How can you seek God and his will in the situations that cause you worry? How might God want to provide a solution for you?

Rebuild

God, our heavenly Father,
thank you for your promise to provide.
May I always seek your kingdom first
when I am worried about money and possessions.
Help me see every need for provision as an opportunity
to draw closer to you and know your goodness.
Amen.

Seek his kingdom, and these other things will
be given you besides.

—Luke 12:31

DAY 17

Follow the Money

No one can serve two masters. He will either hate one and love the other, or be devoted to one and despise the other. You cannot serve God and mammon.

—Jesus to the Pharisees

Read

Money is a major factor in life. We need it to pay our bills, provide for our families, enjoy time with friends, and invest in our retirement. So often it feels as if we can get money wrong or that it just slips through our fingers. Perhaps for that reason, money can provoke many negative emotions: worry, fear, stress, guilt, jealousy, and even anger.

More than anyone who ever lived, Jesus understood money and its place in our lives. Maybe that's why he talked about it so much. It was one of his favorite topics. He wants us to get money right.

In one place he establishes a basic principle about money: "For where your treasure is, there also will your heart be" (Matthew 6:21). Money is a heart issue. Wherever you put your money, your heart naturally goes there along with it. This isn't in itself good or bad; it's just a simple fact of life. Jesus wants us to be intentional with money. As he then taught, "The lamp of the body is the eye. If your eye is sound, your whole body will be filled with light; but if your eye is bad, your whole body will be in darkness. And if the light in you is darkness, how great will the darkness be" (Matthew 6:22–23).

He's telling us that how we see money colors how we see everything else. Viewing money correctly means we're more likely to recognize with clarity how to live our lives. If, on the other hand, we adopt the wrong attitude toward money, we will get just about everything else in life wrong.

That's a pretty broad statement, and maybe you are tempted to discount it. But consider: How many evils are perpetrated in our world every day out of love of money? How many families are wrecked over fights about contested inheritances? What amount of personal pain do we cause ourselves and those we love worrying about money? How much anxiety do we experience because we compare ourselves to people who have more than we do?

Jesus concludes this amazing teaching with another startling but keen observation: "You cannot serve God and mammon [material wealth]" (Matthew 6:24).

The temptation for each of us isn't about serving good or evil, light or darkness, or right or wrong; the temptation is choosing to serve God or money. God wants our hearts, and Jesus said that the number one competitor he faces is our money. If that was true two thousand years ago in a largely agrarian, somewhat impoverished society, how much truer is it for us today? We live in a culture that every day, in every way, tries to convince us, through advertising and marketing, that we need *more*: things that are bigger, better, newer, and faster. If we just drift with the culture and are not intentional about how we use money, it will pull our hearts away from God.

But, while money competes for our hearts and using it selfishly can move our hearts away from God, the inverse is also true. When we use or invest money in the things of God, we can move our hearts in God's direction.

In the Gospel of Luke, we read the story of the tax collector, Zacchaeus. In fact, he wasn't just *any* tax collector but the *chief* tax collector in the city of Jericho and, as a result, a very wealthy man. The only reason a man would choose to be a tax collector was love of money. As we've seen, such officials were considered traitors to their country and outcasts from their faith. The Jewish people detested them because they collected money for the Roman oppressors. This was bad enough, but the job was actually worse.

Tax collectors had to purchase their positions, because such jobs were extremely lucrative and much sought after. They were assigned to collect a prescribed tax for Rome, but then they could add any amount they wanted over and above the Roman tax for their own benefit. It was entirely within their discretion to exact unfair or even excessive amounts, and they had the power of the Roman army behind them. This led, in turn, to widespread corruption. The chief tax collector presided over this criminal enterprise.

Zacchaeus had a pile of money, that's certain. But as much as he had, it wasn't enough. He wasn't satisfied. Excluded from the life of the community due to his personal corruption and the corruption his job supported, he was probably lonely and alone. He wanted something more. How do we know? Well, Luke tells us that Zacchaeus goes out of his way—very much out of his way—just to get a glimpse of Jesus. One day, Jesus visited Jericho, attracting a huge crowd. He also attracted Zacchaeus's attention and interest. We read, "He ran ahead and climbed a sycamore tree in order to see Jesus, who was about to pass that way. When he reached the place, Jesus looked up and said to him, 'Zacchaeus, come down quickly, for today I must stay at your house'" (Luke 19:4–5).

To say the least, it would have been unexpected for a man in Zacchaeus's position to run in the street or climb a tree. Still *more* unexpected that Jesus should stop at that very spot. But most unexpected of all was the proposal to dine together at Zacchaeus's house. Of all the people he could have eaten with in Jericho, of all the people who would have loved to welcome him, Jesus chooses the greedy, crooked tax collector. It was shocking to the crowd. Zacchaeus, however, is delighted and receives him with joy; it is a moment of conversion. And how does Zacchaeus mark this moment? He says to Jesus, "Behold, half of my possessions, Lord, I shall give to the poor, and if I have extorted anything from anyone I shall repay it four times over" (Luke 19:8).

Zacchaeus, who loves money, has a change of heart after meeting Jesus. He discovers a new love, and this discovery leads him to make a bold move. He gives half his fortune to the poor and promises to repay more than he has stolen from others. His resolution to share his fortune with the poor and make restitution to those he defrauded was the sign of Zacchaeus's profound repentance. In turn, it was precisely this resolution that disposed him to God's saving grace. And it marks the beginning of his relationship with the Lord. Jesus responds, "Today salvation has come to this house" (Luke 19:9).

This extreme case proves the rule for everyone. You may not love money the way Zacchaeus did, but using your money properly will move you in God's direction. With the right attitude toward money, we give a part of our hearts back to God. In exchange, God gives us more of his blessing, more of his grace, and more of himself. Seeing money through this lens is a game changer for rebuilding our faith. In order to successfully do that, we have to make a most significant change in attitude, as we'll see tomorrow.

Reflect

What is your natural attitude toward money? What did your family teach you about money? What lessons have you learned from the culture?

When has your heart been moved because of how you spent your money?

In what ways can you use your money to serve God and grow closer to him?

Rebuild

God, our heavenly Father,
we praise you and thank you
for Jesus's clear teaching on money.
Relieve me of any unhealthy attitudes toward money
that distort my view of life and damage my relationships.
May I use my money and possessions
in a way that moves my heart
to the things that matter the most, that matter to you.
Help me to see money in the light of your love.
Through our Lord Jesus Christ, your Son,
who lives with you in the unity of the Holy Spirit.
Amen.

For where your treasure is, there also
will your heart be.

—Matthew 6:21

DAY 18

Be Stewards, Not Owners

In the end, everything has been entrusted to our protection,
and all of us are responsible for it. Be protectors of God's gifts.

—*Pope Francis*

Read

God loves, so God gives to us and provides for us. Our understanding of money and possessions will be healthiest when we
root it in God's love and come to see that we can use money to
move our hearts in God's direction. In addition, Jesus taught two
other key principles that are absolutely crucial to comprehend if
we want to get our money right and use it in a way that moves us
closer to God.

Along with being the greatest preacher and teacher ever,
Jesus was a keen observer of human nature. He reminds us of
obvious truths we tend to forget. He taught, "Do not store up
for yourselves treasure on earth, where moth and decay destroy,
and thieves break in and steal" (Matthew 6:19). Earthly treasure,
all our money and the stuff money can buy, is all only temporary. For any number of reasons, it eventually will pass from our
hands. Sometimes people read that verse from Matthew's gospel
and think Jesus is against money, but it turns out just the opposite is true, as he later said, "Store up treasures in heaven, where
neither moth nor decay destroys, nor thieves break in and steal"
(Matthew 6:20).

Jesus definitely wants us to have treasure. He just wants us to have treasure that will *last*. "Treasure in heaven" is a phrase that Jesus uses quite a few times in the gospels. When it comes to our treasure, we know we can't take it with us, but we can send it on ahead.

In Luke's gospel, Jesus calls such treasure "inexhaustible" (12:33), something that cannot be depleted, a wealth that is never taken away. He may not mean wealth exactly as we think of it, as he is certainly pointing to a value beyond our concept of money. But he's talking about real rewards nonetheless.

To grasp these principles, we're going to look at a parable that often confuses people. Admittedly, it is confusing. The key to understand the parable is not to overthink it. Here's what Luke writes: "Then [Jesus] also said to his disciples, 'A rich man had a steward who was reported to him for squandering his property. He summoned him and said, "What is this I hear about you? Prepare a full account of your stewardship, because you can no longer be my steward"'" (Luke 16:1–2).

Jesus begins this story by introducing us to two characters. One is a man who has so much wealth that he needs someone else to manage it for him. Wealth managers are common in our day, but in antiquity they were rare, suggesting this man had enormous wealth. The other character is the money manager. As a result of his blatant mismanagement and malfeasance, the master decides to terminate his stewardship. At this point, the shrewd steward immediately goes into planning mode: "The steward said to himself, 'What shall I do, now that my master is taking the position of steward away from me? I am not strong enough to dig and I am ashamed to beg. I know what I shall do so that when I am removed from the stewardship, they may welcome me into their homes'" (Luke 16:3–4).

His strategy is all about providing for his future during his remaining time as steward. This is what wise people do. They plan for the future in the knowledge that one day the future *will* be the present. Smart people start planning for retirement early in their careers, knowing there will be a time they can no longer work. Young couples save for the day they can buy their first house. Families make sacrifices in order to finance their dream vacation.

Here's what the steward does to prepare for his future: "He called in his master's debtors one by one. To the first he said, 'How much do you owe my master?' He replied, 'One hundred measures of olive oil.' He said to him, 'Here is your promissory note. Sit down quickly and write one for fifty.' Then to another he said, 'And you, how much do you owe?' He replied, 'One hundred kors of wheat.' [The steward] said to him, 'Here is your promissory note; write one for eighty'" (Luke 16:5–7).

Whose money did the steward give away by reducing the debts? It's not a trick question. The *master's* money. He gave away money that didn't belong to him for his *personal* benefit. Using the master's money, he established a debt of gratitude with his master's creditors that would yield rewards later.

The parable ends this way: "And the master commended the dishonest steward for acting prudently" (Luke 16:8a). The master *commends* the dishonest steward. But he was *dishonest*! Yes! The master doesn't commend the steward for his business ethics or moral character. That's not the purpose of the parable, and it isn't the point. Jesus tells parables that introduce absurd situations and laughable scenarios to entertain his disciples for sure but also to teach certain truths in a way that was very easy to remember. This parable offers two major points about money.

First point: You and I are *stewards*, not *owners*.

In a parable, someone usually represents God and someone usually represents us. You've probably already figured out that the master in this parable is God. We are represented by the steward, because we serve as God's money managers. The money and stuff in your possession don't actually belong to you. It all belongs to God.

The Bible says, "The earth is the LORD's and all it holds, the world and those who dwell in it" (Psalm 24:1). We have just a little bit of time to manage just a little bit of God's money. There was a time before you had the money you now have, and there will be a time when you no longer have it. It has been said that when the fabulously wealthy John D. Rockefeller died, his accountant was asked, "How much did John D. leave?" His accountant replied, "All of it." It was no longer Rockefeller's money.

Second point: Use God's money in your strategic best interest.

Jesus then says, "For the children of this world are more prudent in dealing with their own generation than are the children of light" (Luke 16:8b). People who think this world is all there is, that this life does not impact the next, know how to use money in their best interest according to the standards of the world. Conversely, many Christ followers don't always know how to use money in their best interest according to the standards of eternity. They all too often fail to recognize that worldly wealth is temporary, but it can be exchanged for value that is eternal.

Jesus goes on, "I tell you, make friends for yourselves with dishonest wealth, so that when it fails, you will be welcomed into eternal dwellings" (Luke 16:9). Make friends using your wealth. That sounds funny, but it's not. Make friends using your wealth in the same way the steward made friends with his master's wealth. Be generous with your money. Use your money for the benefit of others. Give away money so that other people come to know Christ. Wise people build their lives on what is eternal and squeeze in what is temporary. They arrange their budgets around giving to God and investing in people, and then they consider everything else. But the important, in fact critical, word in this verse is *when*: "*When* it fails . . ." Inevitably, this world's wealth will fail to be of any use to you at some point.

When you play the game of Monopoly, the fake money holds great value *during the game*. When the game is over, it is useless. It all goes back in the box. If you are a competitive person, you might get excited when you win. But the money's only good for the game. This world's money is Monopoly money. It is valuable for a short period of time, but don't get too attached to it. Use it wisely for your future benefit.

Jesus concludes, "The person who is trustworthy in very small matters is also trustworthy in great ones; and the person who is dishonest in very small matters is also dishonest in great ones. If, therefore, you are not trustworthy with dishonest wealth, who will trust you with true wealth?" (Luke 16:10–11). Money is ultimately a small matter. Compared to faith and hope, friendship and family, and a loving relationship with the living Lord, it is a very small thing. But how we use this small thing is a very big deal. It has eternal consequences. Build your treasure in heaven.

Reflect

What reaction do you have to the idea that you are a steward and not an owner of money and possessions?

What do you think Jesus means by true riches?

How can you remind yourself that your money and possessions are temporary and not eternal?

Rebuild

God, our heavenly Father,
I praise you and thank you for all the blessings
you share with your people in this life.
They are signs to us of your favor and friendship.
Everything you have given, including money,
is a sacred stewardship, not ownership.
Help me embrace that role so that I use money
to invest in others and for my own good

in the light of eternity.
May I one day receive the true riches you intend for me.
I pray through Christ our Lord.
Amen.

> If, therefore, you are not trustworthy
> with dishonest wealth, who will trust
> you with true wealth?

—Luke 16:11

DAY 19

Give in Your Place of Worship

They shall not appear before the LORD empty-handed, but each
with his own gift, in proportion to the blessing which the LORD,
your God, has given to you.

—*Moses*

Read

Alright, here's where the rubber meets the road when it comes
to money and using it in such a way that it moves our hearts to
God. To help us out, we are looking at a passage from the Gospel
of Mark. If you grew up going to church, you may be familiar
with it because from time to time it is read at Mass.

Jesus "sat down opposite the treasury and observed how the
crowd put money into the treasury. Many rich people put in large
sums" (Mark 12:41). This passage takes place during Jesus's final
week alive, just days before his Passion, Death, and Resurrection.
That he sat down and "observed" suggests that Jesus had made
it a point that day to go to the Temple and watch what people
gave. In his final hours, he spent time reflecting on worship and
money. The subject was that important to him.

The "treasury" refers to a court of the Temple complex, east
of the Temple itself. There were thirteen trumpet-shaped bronze
chests located there. As people deposited the metal coins used
for Temple offerings, it was easy to see *and hear* what they were

giving. The clanging of the coins against the bronze chests indicated a little or a lot, which is how we know that "a poor widow also came and put in two small coins worth a few cents" (Mark 12:42).

In that culture widows were often impoverished since they could not inherit their husband's property and they were not permitted to work. Unless they had children to support them, they were destined for poverty, relying on the charity of others. For Mark to specifically note that this widow was poor was to emphasize the point. Of course, no one would have noted or noticed her pittance of an offering. No one, that is, but Jesus.

"Calling his disciples to himself, he said to them, 'Amen, I say to you, this poor widow put in more than all the other contributors to the treasury'" (Mark 12:43). Jesus didn't call the disciples' attention to the wealthy contributing large amounts of money. But when a poor widow puts in two small coins, he uses that moment to teach his disciples a lesson about giving. He says something astounding, which is easy to miss: she gave *more* than all the rest.

On the surface his teaching sounds like utter nonsense. Clearly, in raw numbers, almost everyone gave more money to the treasury than the widow. However, Jesus is teaching his friends and followers to see as God sees and not as human beings do. In God's economy, far more important than the actual dollar amount is the sacrifice the amount represents. God cares about how we steward the money he has given us, and he doesn't compare our amounts to others. This is why Jesus says, "For they have contributed from their surplus wealth, but she, from her poverty, has contributed all she had, her whole livelihood" (Mark 12:44).

The widow gave all of her offering from her *substance*. The wealthy that Jesus observed had given from their *surplus*. It cost the widow far more to give as she did, powerfully demonstrating her dependence on and trust in God. This fact makes Jesus's praise of the woman all the more astounding and all the more interesting. If you read on in this section of Mark's gospel, someone marvels at the Temple's majesty and magnificence, and Jesus replies, "Do you see these great buildings? There will not be one stone left upon another that will not be thrown down" (Mark 13:2).

Jesus knew the Temple was going to be destroyed, which it was, in the Roman siege of Jerusalem in the year AD 70; the bombardment was so intense that the massive stones of the monumental structure literally exploded. He could have stopped the widow and said, "You don't need to do that. God doesn't need your money. I've been watching for a while, and the wealthy people have provided plenty to support the operations of the Temple. Besides, in about forty years this whole complex is coming down. The Romans are going to totally destroy it. So, you just keep your money." Jesus didn't say any of that to her. Why not?

Because Jesus taught that giving is an act of worship when we give to our place of worship. In giving to the place where we regularly attend Mass (which de facto *is* our parish), we honor God. The parish you attend certainly needs money. However, giving to your place of worship is not fundamentally about the parish's need for money, it is about your need to give.

Giving to our place of worship expresses our obedience to God because he asks us to do it. It shows our love for God because our hearts follow our money. Giving where we worship demonstrates gratitude to God because it recognizes him as the owner. When we give in worship, we place our trust in God because it requires sacrifice. Giving in worship is a fuller expression of worship than words alone.

> **Tom:** I was reminded of this a few years ago. I was on vacation at the beach with my family. When we went to Mass on Sunday, I thought I was exempt from having to make any kind of offering because I already give to my parish. Plus, I work for the church, so I don't exactly make a fortune to begin with. However, God

had a different plan. During Mass, I kept hearing his prompting in my heart that I should make a contribution to the offering. I kept arguing with God that I had fulfilled my duty. Besides, I didn't even really like the parish I was visiting. They played canned music, and it was really bad canned music. Yet the Holy Spirit kept working on me until I finally relented, asking God, "How much?"

"All of it. Everything in your wallet."

"Everything?"

"Everything."

Now I had no idea what was in my wallet, but as the basket was passed, I took it out and grabbed all the cash that I had. It amounted to a grand total of fourteen dollars. I had been arguing with God over fourteen dollars! And yet at the same time, it was much more than that. God was teaching me to trust and honor him financially when I worship.

Jesus does not stop the widow because worship and giving go together. And he didn't want to rob her of the blessing she received from giving.

To honor God, we suggest the four Ps of giving from Andy Stanley's *Fields of Gold*. We encourage parishioners to be sure their giving meets all of the following criteria:

- **Planned:** Tom's spontaneous giving on vacation notwithstanding, give thoughtful consideration to what you are going to offer to God. Be intentional about your giving. Make giving to God a line item in your budget.

- **Priority:** Establish giving as priority in your budget. As you are determining what to give back to God, make that your *first* line item. Give to God first.

- **Percentage:** Choose a percentage of your income to give away. We believe *this* is the real game changer when it comes to your relationship with God and a spiritually mature view of money. We encourage people to choose a percentage, keeping in mind the biblical standard of the *tithe*, which is giving 10 percent of your income.

  Tithing is established as the consistent standard for worship giving throughout the Bible beginning in Genesis. In the context of his worship, Abraham gives the priest Melchizedek a tenth of what he has (Genesis 14:18–20). We acknowledge that seems like a high bar for most people (it was for us). So start with any percentage; choose 5 percent, 2 percent, 1 percent. Determine to become a percentage giver.

- **Progressive:** Look to progress in your giving so that God receives a growing percentage of your income as you move closer to the tithe. At the same time, increasingly make financial decisions that allow you to do that.

If you feel nervous and uncomfortable right now, congratulations! That means you are really taking Jesus's teaching and the example of the widow's gift to heart. We know that blessing is on the other side of obedience. Believe that if you start giving to God a percentage of your income as an act of worship, it will take your faith and trust in God to a whole new level.

Reflect

Have you ever felt prompted by God to give? How did you react? What was the result?

How does the concept of giving as worship change your approach to worship?

What is your reaction to the four Ps of giving? Does it make sense? Are you likely to implement it?

Rebuild

God, our heavenly Father,
may I learn from the poor widow,
who gave everything back to you in worship.
May I come to see giving as a way to honor and worship you.
Through your holy name I pray.
Amen.

Calling his disciples to himself, he said to them, "Amen, I say to you, this poor widow put in more than all the other contributors to the treasury."

—Mark 12:43

DAY 20

Give Alms

The rich man who gives to the poor does not
bestow alms but pays a debt.

—*St. Ambrose of Milan*

Read

Money is a spiritual issue. To get money right and use it wisely,
we can learn from Jesus. That means knowing in our heads and
holding in our hearts that God is a provider and we can place
our trust in him. Getting money right means using it to move
our hearts closer to the Lord. It also means accepting that we are
stewards and not owners, thereby building up treasure in heaven.
To get money right, we need to give as an act of worship in our
place of worship. And *then*, it means giving in one other way.

Today, we examine a parable from the Gospel of Luke. Luke
was a physician and an educated man. He wrote his book for
a sophisticated, well-educated, and affluent community. As a
result, Luke features more of Jesus's parables on money than do
the other gospels. He knew his audience had means and therefore needed more instruction on how to use money wisely in the
sight of heaven. The more money we have, the more we need to
pay attention to Jesus's teachings on the subject.

This parable should be read in contrast to the parable we looked
at two days ago. It is the other side of the coin. While the shrewd
servant in the previous story used his money in his own best interest to win friends, the guy we are looking at today does *not*. He, in
fact, makes a huge mistake with the use of his money. That said, this

parable is often used to inflict guilt. But Jesus never leveraged guilt. The point of this parable is not to make us feel guilty but to help us see clearly when it comes to money and act accordingly.

Jesus begins this parable by saying to the Pharisees, "There was a rich man who dressed in purple garments and fine linen and dined sumptuously each day" (Luke 16:19). Today people dress for comfort, as an expression of style, or to meet some established norm, such as a dress code. In the ancient world, people dressed to identify their social status or their job. Wealthy people would dress extravagantly as a sign of their wealth. Purple cloth was the ultimate luxury as it could only be produced from a dye secreted by rare sea snails. So if you wore purple, you had money. The rich man dined sumptuously, the constant feasting a further sign of affluence. In other words, the guy was living the good life as defined by the culture of the time. So, Jesus's listeners are thinking, *Of course; that's what you do if you have money.*

Then we are introduced to a second character: "And lying at his door was a poor man named Lazarus, covered with sores, who would gladly have eaten his fill of the scraps that fell from the rich man's table. Dogs even used to come and lick his sores" (Luke 16:20–21). In just a few words, Jesus, a master storyteller, describes Lazarus's destitution as vividly as he describes the rich man's wealth. Interestingly, this is the only parable where one of the characters is named.

We have two characters living side by side but in two dramatically different situations. Then, something happens that reverses their fortunes. It is something the wealthy man never saw coming but should have, because it is even more predictable than taxes or rush hour traffic: "When the poor man died, he was carried away by angels to the bosom of Abraham. The rich man also died and was buried, and from the netherworld, where he was in torment, he raised his eyes and saw Abraham far off and Lazarus at his side" (Luke 16:22–23).

In an instant, death brings a complete reversal. Lazarus goes to a place of peace and comfort. The wealthy man finds himself in a very different kind of environment. From this purgatory he cries out: "Father Abraham, have pity on me. Send Lazarus to dip the tip of his finger in water and cool my tongue, for I am suffering torment in these flames" (Luke 16:24).

Luke's gospel was written in Greek. The Greek word for *mercy* used here also forms the same root for the word *almsgiving*, which means giving to the poor and under-resourced. This is what the wealthy man could have done with at least some of his money. Now, he pleads for the very mercy he withheld from others. But, we read, "Abraham replied, 'My child, remember that you received what was good during your lifetime while Lazarus likewise received what was bad; but now he is comforted here, whereas you are tormented. Moreover, between us and you a great chasm is established to prevent anyone from crossing'" (Luke 16:25–26).

Even if he wanted to, Abraham can't help the wealthy man; it is simply impossible. It's not even a question of charity, it's about geography. The distance the rich man maintained from the poor man in life is now firmly established. Accepting this sad outcome, the rich man then pleads on behalf of his brothers. Can Lazarus warn them, so they can avoid his fate? "But Abraham replied, 'They have Moses and the prophets. Let them listen to them.' He said, 'Oh no, father Abraham, but if someone from the dead goes to them, they will repent'" (Luke 16:29–30).

Care for the poor wasn't exactly a new idea. Moses and all the prophets taught it as fundamental to the Jewish faith. It was, in fact, one of the distinguishing characteristics of Judaism in the pagan world. This guy's brothers should've known better than to have followed his selfish and self-serving example. But, apparently, they did not. Abraham replied, "If they will not listen to Moses and the prophets, neither will they be persuaded if someone should rise from the dead" (Luke 16:31).

This is a chilling foreshadowing because even after Jesus's Resurrection some people, especially the Pharisees, still refused to believe he was the Son of God. Anyway, the point is, if we are not intentional and disciplined with our money, we will spend it all on ourselves, forgetting the poor. This was true two thousand years ago, and perhaps much truer today in our age of constant consumption and overindulgence. If God has given us more than we need, it is not to spend only on ourselves. We enjoy God's blessing by being a blessing for others. Does this mean you can never have nice things or live well, treat yourself, and splurge from time to time? No. But Christ followers train themselves to see money as a way to increase not only their standard of *living* but also their standard of *giving*.

Jesus's instruction on giving to the poor is clear: they can present themselves in many different ways, and there is no excuse for being ignorant of the poverty around us. In fact, disciples bear a responsibility for knowing about and addressing it.

He does not, however, address many of the questions and concerns that can slow us down and trip us up when it comes to giving, including these: Which are the right charities to give to? What about people who take advantage of others' giving? When is it counterproductive to give money to someone? To be sure, these are important concerns and considerations. They require thought and prayer, but they just shouldn't get in the way of our giving. Evidently, in view of the Lord's uncompromising, unambiguous instruction, when in doubt, we are to *give*.

Money of course is not the only answer to help the under-resourced, but it does play a role. If you are not intentionally giving on a regular basis to charities of your choice, start doing so. Give to organizations that do not just meet people's physical needs but do so motivated by faith. Catholic Relief Services, Catholic Charities USA, or even your own diocesan Catholic Charities are wonderful organizations doing amazing work worthy of your support. Most dioceses offer an annual appeal that assists the needy in your community, another great way to give.

If you already have charities you support, there are ways to go deeper. We talk about planned, priority, percentage, and progressive giving when it comes to worship, and that same model can be applied in almsgiving. Disciples plan and make giving to the poor a priority. They pick a percentage to give away, and then look to progress in their giving.

The mistake of the rich man was he didn't even think about Lazarus. Mindfulness of the poor that leads us to give to the poor is a key way we grow as disciples.

Reflect

Who are some people around you in need? Who is the Lazarus outside your door?

Who are the people in need you naturally feel a tug on your heart to help?

What charities do you currently support? Why do you support them?

Rebuild

God, our heavenly Father,
save me from the blindness of the rich man in the parable.
Teach me to see the people in need around me
as my neighbors,
with whom I can share the resources you have given me.
Amen.

When you give alms, do not let your left hand know what your right is doing, so that your almsgiving may be secret. And your Father who sees in secret will repay you.

—Matthew 6:3–4

DAY 21

Give Cheerfully

Cheerfulness prepares the mind for all noble acts.
—*St. Elizabeth Ann Seton*

Read

The longest discussion on generosity and giving in the New Testament can be found in the eighth and ninth chapters of Paul's Second Letter to the Corinthians. At the time of writing, the church in Jerusalem was suffering greatly because of a severe famine. Moreover, Christians in Jerusalem were already an oppressed minority, ostracized from society. No longer having a place within their Jewish families as they came to faith in Christ, they were also held in suspicion by the Romans, whose gods they rejected. So at this point, their needs were real and their suffering acute. To address the situation, Paul and others rallied Christians in cities throughout the Roman Empire for their support.

Particularly, he invites the Corinthians, an affluent community, to contribute to the Jerusalem church. And he begins his pitch in this way: "We want you to know, brothers, of the grace of God that has been given to the churches of Macedonia, for in a severe test of affliction, the abundance of their joy and their profound poverty overflowed in a wealth of generosity on their part" (2 Corinthians 8:1–2).

Even though the Christians in Macedonia possessed only modest wealth, Paul points out that they were among the first to help the Christians in Jerusalem, giving *above* their means.

In fact, he continues, the church in Macedonia actually *asked* to give. They wanted to give. The impression is that Paul anticipates the *reluctance* of the Corinthians to give.

In a subsequent verse Paul tries another approach: "Now as you excel in every respect, in faith, discourse, knowledge, all earnestness, and in the love we have for you, may you excel in this gracious act also" (2 Corinthians 8:7). The people of Corinth prided themselves on excellence. In the Roman Empire, they enjoyed a reputation for the production of world-class luxury goods, specializing in leather products and decorative mirrors, which were expensive and much sought after. Paul invites them to also take pride in giving in an exceptional way. He offers other reasons to give generously in this chapter, which you can read for yourself. But we are going to skip ahead to the next chapter, where Paul continues to make his case: "Consider this: whoever sows sparingly will also reap sparingly, and whoever sows bountifully will also reap bountifully" (2 Corinthians 9:6). When a farmer sows seed, he knows that his harvest will be in direct proportion to the seed he has sown. Sow a little seed and at harvest time there will only be a modest yield. Sow bountifully, with plenty of seed, and there will be a greater harvest. It is a simple concept that Paul applies to our giving and generosity.

Ultimately, we discover two mentalities when it comes to money and other resources. The first proposes a *scarcity mindset* that says, "We're in a closed system, competing with one another for very limited resources." The scarcity mentality leads us to believe that when I give to others, I am impoverished and diminished. St. Paul suggests a different attitude when it comes to giving, advocating an *abundance mindset*. This attitude recognizes we are in not a *closed* system but an *open* one, an ever-widening circle of resources. It understands God has not left us on our own in a strictly competitive environment. He is with us, and he is a giver, always ready to share his grace and blessings.

The abundance mindset says that giving to others is not an exercise in loss but rather an *investment* that opens us up to receive *more* of God's blessing in our lives. This is why Paul compares giving to sowing seeds for a harvest. The scarcity mindset sows sparingly and reaps only a modest return from giving. The abundance mindset sows bountifully and likewise reaps bountifully.

> **Tom:** These words from Paul never cease to challenge me. At times I look at the gifts I give back to God in worship or to support the poor and think, *I could do so much with that money. I need to remodel my kitchen, my garage needs a new roof, two of the kids now need braces, and we definitely need a new car.* With eight kids, a big house, a dog, and a cat, there are always *needs;* the neediness never goes away. But in different ways that's true for everyone, and *still* God asks us to give.

Paul continues to challenge: "Each must do as already determined, without sadness or compulsion, for God loves a *cheerful giver*" (2 Corinthians 9:7, emphasis added). In one of the most famous verses in scripture, Paul reveals the key to giving. He tells the Corinthians to be *intentional* about their gift, to give not because they feel compelled to give but to give *cheerfully*, knowing that giving expands our lives. God delights when we give joyfully, because when we *give* we *grow*.

"Moreover, God is able to make every grace abundant for you, so that in all things, always having all you need, you may have an abundance for every good work" (2 Corinthians 9:8). Adopt an abundance mentality and give cheerfully, knowing that your giving does not go unnoticed by God. In turn, God can help you abound in good works. Wherever God gives us a *vision* for our lives, he gives a *provision*. He provides for what he wants us to accomplish, whether it is to raise a family, run a business, or pursue an education. Giving opens us up to that provision. After all, as Paul writes:

> The one who supplies seed to the sower and bread for food will supply and multiply your seed and increase the harvest of your righteousness.
> You are being enriched in every way for all generosity, which through us produces thanksgiving to God, for the administration of this public service is not only supplying the needs of the holy ones but is also overflowing in many acts of thanksgiving to God. (2 Corinthians 9:10–12)

Paul explains the virtuous cycle that follows from giving. God gives us money and resources. Gratefully, therefore cheerfully, we take those gifts and sow seeds by giving to people in need, giving to help our brothers and sisters in Christ, and giving so that others will know him. In the process, we increase in righteousness. Oftentimes, God then gives us even more resources so that we, in turn, can give even more generously. Finally, our giving overflows into worship and thanksgiving to God, bringing further blessings as the process begins again.

Paul concludes his teaching on generosity with a final note: "Thanks be to God for his indescribable gift!" (2 Corinthians 9:15). The ability to give is an *indescribable gift* because when we give cheerfully, we are acting like God.

Reflect

Do you tend to have an abundance mindset or a scarcity mindset? Why do you think you lean toward one mindset or the other?

Who has provided for you? Whom do you need to thank God for because they have given generously in your life?

When have you given cheerfully and found yourself grateful for the opportunity to give to others? How has this week's focus on tithing and giving affected your attitude toward giving?

Rebuild

God, our heavenly Father,
I praise and thank you
that you have called me to be a cheerful giver,
embracing an abundance mentality.
Heal me of my scarcity mindset
that believes I have to compete with others for resources.
Allow me to see you as my Provider,
and help me to be a provider for others.
Amen.

Each must do as already determined, without sadness or compulsion, for God loves a cheerful giver.

—2 Corinthians 9:7

WEEK FOUR

Engage in Christian Community

DAY 22

Don't Be Alone

Christ wishes the Christian community to be a body that is perfect because we work together toward a single end.
—*St. Katherine Drexel*

Read

Tom: God has a sense of humor. It is ironic the two of us are writing about engaging in Christian community because, before we worked in a parish, we were never particularly interested in the community aspects of our Catholic faith.

Father Michael: Tom and I both went to the same Catholic university. While we went at different times, we shared a common experience. Though we were never-miss-a-Sunday churchgoers, we didn't like the style of the Masses on campus. There were many to choose from, but they all tended toward the touchy-feely variety, with extended introductions, hand-holding during the Our Father, and lots of hugging at the Sign of Peace. Definitely not our style. For my part, I developed the weekly habit of walking more than a mile off campus to the local parish church, which happened to be the cathedral church, for

Sunday Mass. The place was huge and often not at all crowded, and it was easy to sit in the back all by myself. Years later I was surprised to learn Tom had adapted exactly the same practice when he was in college. For both of us, going to church was definitely all about *alone* time.

Our experiences remind us of the story of a visitor to a certain parish church. When it came time for the Sign of Peace, he turned to the elderly lady in the pew behind him; her head piously bowed, eyes closed, and hands firmly clenched in prayer. The visitor warmly greeted her, "Peace be with you," as he stretched out his hand. The church lady opened her eyes and, looking up, snapped, "I don't go in for that s***."

We kind of grew up feeling the same way. We didn't go in for community. Faith is personal and private; that's what we thought. And while there might be other people at Mass, our worship is one-on-one time with God. Of course, quiet time and personal time are great. Alone time is important, but when it comes to faith (and life in general), it is not good for us to *be all alone*. It is not healthy for us.

We see this so clearly displayed in the book of Genesis. When God created the world and everything in it, he pronounced it *good*. He creates light and pronounces that it is good. He creates the sea and dry land, trees and plants, and he pronounces them good. When God had the world as he wanted it, everything was good: no death or disease, no war or conflict, no hunger or homelessness, no country music.

God creates a complete paradise, the perfect environment for man. Genesis tells us, "The LORD God then took the man and settled him in the garden of Eden, to cultivate it and care for it" (Genesis 2:15). Work is yet another gift from God. Like everything else in paradise, even work is good. All is good. This makes the next verse surprising: "The LORD God said: It is *not good* for the man to be alone. I will make a helper suited to him" (Genesis 2:18, emphasis added).

Despite all that Adam has going for him—a good job, a beautiful home, and a great relationship with God—something is still wrong. And for the first time in all creation, God pronounces something "not good." God identifies a problem in Adam's life that even Adam at this point does not truly understand. This is our reality. We don't always see the problems in our lives. We can't necessarily recognize when something is missing that we truly need. And what does God see that Adam doesn't see? He sees that it is not good for Adam to be alone.

As we reflected on Day 15, there is no loneliness in God. God does not know loneliness because God is not alone. God is a community of three persons—Father, Son, and Holy Spirit—who are continually loving one another and glorifying one another for all eternity. God knows the value of community, the value of having a relationship with someone of the same nature.

God observes Adam's situation and pronounces it *not good* because it is lacking in a major way. Even though Adam has a strong relationship with God, it's not enough. That almost sounds blasphemous because so often we are told that all we need is God. However, that's not what God says. God says that as human beings, we need more. We need relationships with other people as well.

Spiritual growth and health require more than simply seeking a solid relationship with God. You will not grow closer to God and you will not become the person God has created you to be by just spending time with God in personal prayer. Prayer is essential, but it's not enough. To grow as a Christ follower, you need relationships with others who also want to follow Christ.

The strength and power of believers coming together is amazing. We see this reflected in physics and in nature. Redwood trees can grow to be about 350 feet high; for comparison, that's a thirty-five-story building. You might think that trees like that would have deep roots. But they don't. Their roots are only five or six feet deep. But what they lack in depth they make up for in width, as they extend far out to other trees. They thrive in thick groves where their roots can intertwine and fuse together, forming a solid foundation for all the trees in the grove.

Canada geese fly south for the winter, but you usually don't see a goose flying alone. They fly together in V formations. Geese flying together can travel 70 percent farther than a goose flying alone. These migratory birds instinctively understand that if they want to go farther faster, they need to fly in a group formation, called a skein. Evolution and instinct have ensured that they do not try to survive and thrive on their own.

As humans, we are not always so smart. Or we are too smart for our own good and think we can do life by ourselves. We may not see the inherent challenge of trying to do life on our own, but God does: "So the LORD God formed out of the ground all the wild animals and all the birds of the air, and he brought them to the man to see what he would call them; whatever the man called each living creature was then its name. The man gave names to all the tame animals, all the birds of the air, and all the wild animals" (Genesis 2:19–20a).

Adam is alone, and God begins to address the problem by presenting the animals of creation to him to see if any could serve as a suitable partner. "But none proved to be a helper suited to the man" (Genesis 2:20b). Now wait a minute: Didn't God know that none of the animals would satisfy Adam's need for companionship? Of course he did. *He* knew that, but *Adam* didn't. Through this parade of animals, God deepens Adam's desire for true connection. As each of the animals disappoint, Adam learns more about his need for intimacy in which he can know another and be known. God helps Adam discover what he is lacking in his life, so he can recognize God's gift when it is given to him.

So when Adam is finally, keenly aware of his need for *human* companionship, God goes to work to fix the problem:

> So the LORD God cast a deep sleep on the man, and
> while he was asleep, he took out one of his ribs and
> closed up its place with flesh. The LORD God then
> built the rib that he had taken from the man into a
> woman. When he brought her to the man, the man
> said:
>
> "This one, at last, is bone of my bones
>   and flesh of my flesh." (Genesis 2:21–23)

Adam instantly recognizes what he's been missing. His sigh of "at last" suggests deep relief as well as new exuberance and enthusiasm for life—all because he now has a relationship.

In *The Four Loves*, C. S. Lewis writes, "As soon as we are fully conscious we discover loneliness. We need others physically, emotionally, intellectually; we require them if we are to know anything, even ourselves." We need others to know *ourselves*, and we need others to know *God*. Until we internalize this truth and embrace the third one of our STEPS by engaging in Christian community, we stunt our spiritual growth, keeping us from becoming all God has created us to be.

Reflect

On a scale of one to five, how much of a problem is loneliness for you? Why did you assign the number you did?

When have you experienced relief that someone understood you and your point of view?

Do you tend to see faith as a solitary exercise, or are you more open to community?

Rebuild

God, our heavenly Father,
you have designed me and formed me,
and I give thanks that I am fearfully, wonderfully made.
In your wonderful design
you have created me for connections and community,
which I need to grow in faith.
Bring people of faith into my life to help me grow in faith.
All these things I pray through Christ, our Lord.
Amen.

The LORD God said: It is not good for the man to be alone. I will make a helper suited to him.

—Genesis 2:18

DAY 23

Join a Parish

The parish church is the heart of the Church.
—*United States Conference of Catholic Bishops*

Read

Everyone knows it is not good for us to be alone when considering nearly every area of our lives. And yet, when it comes to our faith life, there is a growing phenomenon in Western culture in which many seem to think they don't need the community of the Church. When we started our work in the parish more than twenty-five years ago, the pattern of declining attendance and engagement was in its early stages. Since then, the decline has dramatically accelerated. According to Gallup, in 2020 just 47 percent, or less than half, of US adults belonged or had a loose connection to a church, synagogue, or mosque, down more than twenty percentage points from the turn of the century ("U.S. Church Membership Falls Below Majority for First Time," Gallup, March, 29, 2021). The post-COVID-19 experience of many parishes suggests continued decline.

Increasingly, many people believe they can connect to God completely all alone and on their own. They contend that they don't need the Church to talk to God or be a good person. They argue that their faith is private and their prayer is personal. Some have given up on the communal aspects of the Church because they've been turned off by hypocritical leaders or infighting among church members and would just rather have nothing to do with such communities. Still others find a sense of community in their circle of friends or through sports and recreational programs, rendering church community seemingly unnecessary. And post-COVID-19, even many former churchgoers have simply fallen out of the practice of church attendance.

> **Tom:** Just yesterday I heard a well-known media figure call all of Christianity "satire." If you observe our culture, you can easily and quickly conclude that the Church is irrelevant. The evidence and the experience are around us all the time. It can begin to feel as if no one goes to church anymore. A good friend of mine, Bob, works in a large corporate setting with many other high-profile professionals. Recently, a colleague stepped into his office and closed the door. He wanted to know if it was true that Bob actually goes to church.

Definitely, this is a developing phenomenon in our culture, and maybe it is one to which you relate. Interestingly, this is not just a modern phenomenon. The writer of Hebrews had to remind the early Church about the importance of gathering: "We should not stay away from *our assembly*, as is the custom of some, but encourage one another, and this all the more as you see the day drawing near" (Hebrews 10:25, emphasis added). Though its authorship is contested, the letter was addressed primarily to Jewish converts who were being tempted away from Christianity and back to Judaism—and, in the process, neglecting the community and the fellowship of the Church.

The Church is not a building, at least in the original sense. The Latin word *ecclesia* is a translation of the Greek *ekalein*, referring to an assembly or convocation of people rather like a town hall meeting. Throughout scripture, God commands his people to gather in just such an assembly to celebrate his providence and his goodness, *together*. In Leviticus 23, God tells the Israelites, "The seventh day is a sabbath of complete rest, a declared holy day; you shall do no work. It is the LORD's sabbath wherever you dwell" (Leviticus 23:3). Other translations say it is a day of sacred assembly.

The Old Testament Sabbath established the foundation for the New Testament Sunday celebration. In the Acts of the Apostles, we are told, "All who believed were together and had all things in common. . . . Every day they devoted themselves to meeting together in the temple area" (Acts 2:44, 46). Whenever we gather with others—at sporting events, the theater, or a rally—it definitely touches our spirit. The experience can even impact who we are and how we look at life. God commands we gather together as his people because he knows we need this kind of fellowship for our spiritual nourishment and emotional health. We *grow* spiritually when we meet with God's people for the purpose of praising God. Do it on a consistent basis, and it can enrich your soul. At the same time, the assembly stands as a living witness to God in the world.

We are to gather together in assembly or community. And it needs to be a *specific* community. Why? Because nothing gets dynamic, nothing will change your heart and impact your life, until it gets specific. A specific assembly, the parish church, is where Catholics commit to *how* they are going to grow in faith and positively impact the community for Christ. We gather together to align ourselves with other Christ followers on how to change the world for good and for God.

The Church is the assembly of God's people. But the relationship is actually tighter than any other kind of assembly. In the famous story of St. Paul's conversion, he hears the voice of the Lord say to him, "Saul, Saul, why are you persecuting me?" (Acts 9:4). Jesus didn't ask, "Why are you persecuting my friends and followers?" (which Paul was). He takes Paul's persecution of the Church personally, as an attack on his person.

Later, in one of his letters to the Corinthians, Paul says that as members of the Church, together with other believers, we are "Christ's body." This isn't an analogy; in some mystical way we truly are connected to other Christ followers. According to Paul, the body needs the other members: "As a body is one though it has many parts, and all the parts of the body, though many, are one body, so also Christ. For in one Spirit we were all baptized into one body" (1 Corinthians 12:12–13a). Paul goes on to explain that the different parts of the body *need* each other. Your eyes need the ears to hear. Ears require eyes to see. Eyes and ears rely on legs to actually get anywhere. In the same way that each part of the body needs the other parts to be healthy and whole, we need other members of the Body of Christ.

This mutual care requires a specific community of Christ followers, or it's just wishful thinking. There are many people who say they love the Church. And yet, they don't belong to any specific parish. They drift from parish to parish, "church shopping," in search of the most convenient Mass time, preferred music, or favorite preacher. It's not good for their souls, and it is not good for the community of believers.

God's vision for the Church is not to be a sacramental filling station or a mere consumer exchange. His vision is to grow committed communities of believers to be a visible, vibrant sign of his love to the world while building the personal faith of those assembled. The STEPS of discipleship build up both the local community of faith and the individual believer. While the world often pits the individual against the greater good, the paradox of Christian faith is that it grows both community and individual faith. The Christian faith builds the group and helps individuals become who God created them to be.

We'll go even further: You probably cannot become fully who God created you to be without belonging and committing to a local community of faith. Our souls need a local community where we are known, loved, and cared for and where we can know love and care for others. We need to love a specific Body of Christ and commit to it. And the Church needs people to commit to specific communities. Any company or organization that is successful or great has people who love it. In his book *Orthodoxy*, G. K. Chesterton said, "Men did not love Rome because she was great. She was great because they had loved her." The overall health of the Church and your faith will grow when you decide to commit to a specific parish and when you decide to love it.

Reflect

Who were the people who were helpful in your faith formation when growing up?

When have you seen the benefit of gathering with other Christ followers? How have such gatherings nourished your soul and built up your faith?

Are you part of a faith community? If so, what do you love about it? If not, what makes you resist being part of a faith community?

Rebuild

God, our heavenly Father,
you have given me my local parish community
to build up my personal faith and relationship with you.
Help me love this community and love my fellow parishioners.
Through Christ our Lord.
Amen.

As a body is one though it has many parts, and all the parts of the body, though many, are one body, so also Christ. For in one Spirit we were all baptized into one body.

—1 Corinthians 12:12–13a

DAY 24

Find Friends in Faith

Friendship (as the ancients saw) can be a school of virtue; but
also (as they did not see) a school of vice. It's ambivalent. It
makes good men better and bad men worse.

—C. S. Lewis

Read

You are not meant to follow Jesus on your own. You cannot
become a fully devoted follower of Christ apart from his Body,
the Church. It just can't be done. To more successfully follow
Jesus and win the rewards of the kingdom of heaven, you need
to be a part of his team that is the Church. And, as we also discussed yesterday, you need to belong and commit to a *specific*
parish because that is where the Church lives.

But even that is not enough. To keep growing as a Christ follower requires other, specific Christians whom you know, who
know you, and who can consistently support you. We've learned
this works best in a faith-sharing community, which at our parish, we call "small groups."

What is a small group? Well, first of all, it is *small*: six to twelve
people who get together on a regular basis, usually weekly, to discuss *not* facts about faith but the experience and the pursuit of it.
Small groups come in various forms and take different directions
depending on the participants. We like to say small groups discuss the Bible, but they are *not* Bible studies. They support one

another, but they are *not* support groups; they pray together, but they are *not* prayer groups.

Instead, groups blend all three together as we meet with other Christ followers to understand where God is working in one another's lives. In groups we help each other process how we follow Jesus within the day-to-day choices we make and directions we take. Groups are places to share how the truth of the gospel is working in the daily experience of members. They provide an opportunity to tell our stories and, in the process, come to a greater personal understanding of what has happened in our lives. More than that, groups provide an environment; they create a space to actually have conversations about faith. And, for many Catholics, that in itself is a unique experience. But we've actually found they can be a game-changing opportunity for people to step up in their faith.

Here are three reasons you need to get in a small group.

First, when we're talking about small groups, we're talking about *friends in faith*. Peer pressure is not just a middle school phenomenon. As human beings, we are influenced by the people whom we spend time with. Don't believe us? Just notice how you start using the same words and phrases people around you use. Reflect for a moment on the many times you've made a decision based on how other people will think or react. In fact, study after study shows that our financial status and physical well-being are dramatically impacted by the people who surround us.

Your friends *will* determine the direction, and sometimes the quality, of your life. We are being influenced all the time by the people around us. We can either have that influence positively or negatively impact our faith life. Without friends in faith, we're on our own when it comes to resisting peer pressure so that we can grow as followers of Christ. With friends in faith, our relationships work for us. Proverbs says it this way, "Walk with the wise and you become wise, but the companion of fools fares badly" (Proverbs 13:20).

Friendship, though, is so much more than staying out of trouble. While we don't technically need friendship for survival, friendship adds value and joy to our lives. In small groups, we meet companions on our spiritual journey who can grow to become our friends. Groups are the pathway to friendship.

In one place St. Paul writes, "With such affection for you, we were determined to share with you not only the gospel of God, but our very selves as well, so dearly beloved had you become to us" (1 Thessalonians 2:8). We all have "friends" in our life who are friends of convenience, friends formed by mere proximity or affinity, and friends springing from shared seasons of life. But rare is the friendship born of faith. Something powerful happens when we find people whose company we enjoy and who can help us grow in our relationship with Christ.

Second reason you need a small group: groups are a place where you can be strengthened and encouraged by other people's faith. In his letter to the Romans, Paul writes, "For I long to see you, that I may share with you some spiritual gift so that you may be strengthened, that is, that you and I may be mutually encouraged by one another's faith, yours and mine" (Romans 1:11–12). Paul looked forward to visiting the church in Rome so he could learn from them and be encouraged by them. Think about Paul and his story. This guy was a spiritual giant. Knowing the Hebrew Scriptures from beginning to end, he also had a complete command of classical philosophy, enabling him to effectively debate with the greatest Jewish scholars and Greek philosophers. He was a linguist and moved comfortably in different countries and cultures. Writing roughly half the New Testament, he established church communities all over the known world. He willingly suffered stoning, beating, and a shipwreck so that others would know Jesus. And, above all, he had a personal encounter with the risen Lord.

Yet as epic as Paul's journey had been, as staggeringly accomplished as he was, and as towering as his faith stood, he told the Romans he *needed* to learn from their faith. He needed their faith to encourage and strengthen him. And if Paul needed to be encouraged by others' faith, then we do too.

Groups provide the environment where you can learn from other people's faith. No matter how mature you are, or think you are, and regardless of how long you've been a practicing Catholic or active in your parish, you have something to learn from others. Likewise, however fresh or tentative your faith, you have something to share with others.

In his chapter on friendship in *The Four Loves*, C. S. Lewis writes, "If, of three friends (A, B, and C), A should die, then B loses not only A but 'A's part in C', while C loses not only A but 'A's part in B'. In each of my friends there is something that only some other friend can fully bring out. By myself I am not large enough to call the whole man into activity; I want other lights than my own to show all his facets."

This applies to our relationship with God. If, by myself, I cannot draw out or truly reflect another finite human being, then how much more is this true about an infinite God? How much *more* do we need one another to learn about and come closer to God? When we don't learn about other people's encounters with God, we actually limit our own relationship with him. Discussions in a group help us come to know God in a way we simply can't know him on our own. Is it not possible that in heaven we will be with all the saints, learning from one another about who God is? Why not start practicing now?

The third reason you need to be part of a small group is that conversion and life change are all part of Christian living. We are not yet who God has created us to be. We all have faults and failures we need to walk away from and leave behind. Each of us has rough edges to our character that can be chiseled away and polished over. We have thought patterns that should be corrected. Small groups provide an environment where we slowly but surely learn new patterns of thinking and form better habits for living. The more we have conversations with others who follow Christ, the more we become like him. As Proverbs says, "Iron is sharpened by iron; one person sharpens another" (Proverbs 27:17).

God made us to learn from other people's experiences and examples. When people sit in a circle and share their stories, they grow in an understanding of how life works. It is no mere coincidence that conversation and conversion have the same roots in Latin. Throughout our lives, our conversations change us. And sometimes they convert us. The power of small groups comes from forming relationships in which *conversations* lead to *conversion*.

Reflect

Who are the people who sharpen you and help you grow? Are they people who help you grow in faith?

Do you have close friends with whom you can share both the Gospel and what is happening in your life?

Of the three reasons given for joining a small group (friends in faith, encouragement from others' faith, and conversion), which one most appeals to you?

Rebuild

God, our heavenly Father,
thank you for the great gift of friendship.
Give me friends to walk with me in faith.
In the most high name of Jesus, we pray.
Amen.

Iron is sharpened by iron; one person sharpens another.

—Proverbs 27:17

DAY 25

Develop Relationships That Support Other Relationships

*You are my companion and must walk with me,
for if we hold together no earthly power can withstand us.*

—*St. Dominic, upon meeting St. Francis*

Read

Relationships would be easy if it wasn't for people.

People bring drama. Dealing with people can be difficult, sometimes *very* difficult. People in front of us at the grocery store checkout, nosy neighbors in our neighborhood association, and the loud family at the next table can all infuriate us. In our encounters with others, we inevitably experience the full range of unpleasant emotions: anger, annoyance, bewilderment, confusion, displeasure, exasperation, irritation, and vexation. Did we miss anything?

Our general frustrations (okay, we missed that one) with people can prevent us from engaging in Christian community. You might respond to our challenge to connect with a small group by thinking, *I don't need any more people in my life. I don't need any more drama.* We can understand that point of view; however, Jesus himself addressed the drama of human relationships and had a prescription for it. Many of his teachings specifically speak to the point that dealing with other people can be difficult. We see these teachings throughout the gospels, but especially in one we'll look at more closely today.

Before we get to that teaching, we must remember that Jesus knows what he is talking about. He is the wisest person who ever lived, and he speaks with authority on all of life, including how relationships work. And he doesn't speak from a life of easy relationships. Like us, he had difficulties with his family members (and then some): at one point, in response to his teaching and preaching, his relatives tried to shut down his ministry (Mark 3:21). Like us, he experienced conflict with neighbors. After he preached his first sermon, they tried to kill him (Luke 4:29–30). Like us, he had challenges with his coworkers: the apostles were constantly fighting with one another and misunderstanding what he was trying to teach them (Mark 9:33–34). Like us, he faced criticism and conflict as he sought to achieve results. He was opposed by the religious authorities who constantly criticized him and worked to discredit him (Mark 3:22).

So when Jesus tells us how to deal with the drama that comes from human relationships, he speaks with wisdom, understanding, knowledge, insight, and experience. *Like* us, he faced conflict with others, but *unlike* us, he never got drawn into the drama. He didn't allow other people's actions to dictate his reactions.

> **Father Michael:** I am often reminded of this fact when flying. Not long ago I had a particularly unpleasant experience. I was fortunate to get an aisle seat, but the plane was still boarding and sure enough someone sat in the seat next to me and was instantly a problem. A big guy, he kind of spread out beyond his assigned space, taking complete command of the armrest. I didn't say anything, but I was annoyed. Then, it turned out, the guy couldn't sit still. He was moving around, fussing with junk in his carry-on, balancing snacks and a

coffee on his foldout tray table (which I feared he was going to spill on me), and constantly hitting buttons on the screen in front of him in a manic manner. All the while my annoyance was growing. Finally, I was fully determined to let him know how annoyed I was when I heard, "Hi, Fr. White!" One of the boarding passengers was a parishioner. I decided not to make a scene.

It is an experience we all have. Metaphorically, people push us off our armrest. They can offend us just by being around. Or we have to deal with other people's hurts and hang-ups, with their faults and flaws. And *our* feelings get hurt in the process, we get offended. It's the human condition in our fallen world. The question is not *if* people will negatively affect us but how to deal with it effectively as a Christ follower *when* they negatively affect us.

Jesus speaks to this in the so-called Sermon on the Plain: "Love your enemies, do good to those who hate you, bless those who curse you, pray for those who mistreat you" (Luke 6:27–28). Sometimes our enemies are the people outside our organization, the competition, or they're just faceless critics we don't even know. But sometimes, maybe more often, our enemies are in our own household, workplace, or community. We tend to fight most consistently with the people close at hand. Proximity brings conflict whether it be with an ungrateful, whiny child; a nagging, needy parent; an unhelpful sibling; a coworker who actually undercuts our efforts; or a classmate who bullies and harasses us. These can be the real enemies in our lives.

To succeed in those relationships and grow in goodness, Jesus teaches that you've got to love your enemy. Choosing to love turns you into the hero who is free to do good rather than the helpless victim or the angry revenger. He challenges us to actively love the person and let the love of God, rather than their behavior, dictate our actions.

Jesus says love your enemy, then he gives very specific illustrations on *how* you can love your enemy. *Do good for them.* When someone is opposing you, choose to find a way to serve them, assist them, and help them. Do good for them and bless them. In other words, speak positive words over them. Pray for them.

It is here Jesus says something you have heard so many times before that it just sounds like a platitude. But we cannot let it become so. He says, "Do to others as you would have them do to you" (Luke 6:31). It's the so-called Golden Rule. Whatever action or reaction you would want from someone else in any given situation, reverse engineer it and act accordingly. It's so simple and so challenging, like so much of the Christian life.

Then he continues: "But rather, love your enemies and do good to them, and lend expecting nothing back; then your reward will be great and you will be children of the Most High, for he himself is kind to the ungrateful and the wicked. Be merciful, just as [also] your Father is merciful" (Luke 6:35–36). Expect nothing back; empty your expectations. Do good for the sake of doing good and being like your heavenly Father. God shows us mercy and grants us grace and favor, expecting and getting absolutely nothing in return. Ever. Be like that. Why? Simple. It's always the way to most efficiently and effectively handle a difficult situation. When one party chooses to show mercy and act generously, it more often than not reverses the entire dynamic; hearts are touched, and minds are changed.

The attribution theory in psychology holds that we tend to excuse our own failures as mistakes that are out of character. At the same time, we tend to blame other people's failures due to malice and bad character. Jesus reverses that, telling us to do the opposite.

This brings us to today's point. Putting aside any spiritual consolation or inspiration, small groups bring an incredibly helpful practical benefit. Small groups are relationships that support your *other* relationships. We get into groups so that other Christ followers can help us apply the Golden Rule to our relationships. The Golden Rule is countercultural, the way of God's kingdom and not the way of the world. We need voices speaking into our life that remind us about Jesus's teaching when we inevitably encounter problems in our daily experiences. We need a safe place where we can process those conflicts in a Christian context.

Think about it: in your work relationships and your family relationships, you have to be "on." People want and need something *from* you. At work you have to maintain a certain level of professionalism in whatever role you hold. The relationships you form professionally are intended to serve the business of your organization. At home there is most definitely a certain performance—as a parent, spouse, or sibling—that is expected of you. Those relationships can be challenging. We need support in managing them in a positive way.

Small groups are a place where, other than being honest and actively listening to others, there are no expectations on you. You can bring your struggles and challenges with other people to the group: people who have no vested interest in the situation and the players but a solid interest in you. Your group can be people who are *for you*, so you can be better at being for others.

Reflect

Is there someone you are struggling to get along with right now? What would it look like to apply the Golden Rule to that relationship?

Who are the people helping you to process struggles with others? Whom do you help?

How would having a small Christian community help you grow to be a better person in the roles you play?

Rebuild

God, our heavenly Father,
thank you for your Son's teachings on relationships.
Practicing the Golden Rule,
may I treat others as I would have them treat me
through difficulties and challenges.
I pray this through Jesus Christ, who is Lord forever and ever.
Amen.

[Jesus said,] "Do to others as you would
have them do to you."

—Luke 6:31

DAY 26

Let Others Believe for You

A companion is but another self.

—*St. Clement I*

Read

To become fully devoted followers of Christ, we need other people to challenge us and help us grow. We need others to remind us to respond with love when the people around us are not acting in very loving ways. The analogy of a charcoal fire is often used when it comes to the Christian life. Put the coals together, and they produce enough heat to cook. Take one away from the other coals, and the heat from the single coal quickly dissipates. If we live separated from Christian community for too long, our faith can grow cold.

But not only do we need Christian community to keep the fire of faith alive in our hearts, sometimes we need it just to *stay* in the faith at all. At times, it actually becomes difficult to believe in the goodness of God. Faith and trust in God ebbs and flows, and it can take a major dive like the stock market after a catastrophe. And when that happens, we need help. What does that help look like? A passage from the second chapter of Mark's gospel might offer some assistance.

"When Jesus returned to Capernaum after some days, it became known that he was at home" (Mark 2:1). Jesus returns to Capernaum, the town that served as his home base for most of his time in public ministry. The last time he was there he left behind crowds of people who wanted his attention and, most urgently, his healing touch. He left because he wanted to widen the reach of his preaching and teaching throughout that region of Galilee. Now that he was back, word quickly spreads through the town of about 1,500 citizens. And just as quickly, a crowd forms.

"Many gathered together so that there was no longer room for them, not even around the door, and he preached the word to them. They came bringing to him a paralytic carried by four men. Unable to get near Jesus because of the crowd, they opened up the roof above him. After they had broken through, they let down the mat on which the paralytic was lying" (Mark 2:2–4). Four men bring a paralyzed man on a stretcher. They want Jesus to heal their friend. But then they can't get near him because of the large number of people, which included just about the whole town. At that point they could have just given up, acknowledging that it just wasn't meant to be. And they might have been forgiven for going back home for the evening to try again another day. The instinct for most people when we do hit an obstacle is to give up and accept defeat. Carrying on can seem pointless and trying to move forward a waste of time.

Instead, they persevere in their resolve to reach Jesus. Climbing up on the roof, they create an opening, probably by removing the clay roofing tiles, and then they lower their friend down, right in front of Jesus. The paralytic had no ability whatsoever to get to Jesus. His friends did. They had the ability and the opportunity, but they also had the perseverance. As we will see, faith requires perseverance (Day 35).

Whatever his reaction to their unexpected approach, Jesus was clearly impressed by their perseverance, a reflection of their confidence and faith in him: "When Jesus saw their faith, he said to the paralytic, 'Child, your sins are forgiven'" (Mark 2:5). Jesus *saw their faith*. Whose faith does Jesus see? He sees the faith of the paralytic's *friends*. He sees that they persevered to bring their friend to Jesus.

Ever notice that it is often easier to do something for someone else than it is for yourself? There are good things that you know you should do that would be good for you, but you don't do them. However, if someone asks you to help them, you readily respond. Or when it comes to our problems, sometimes we are so much in the weeds of them we can't see the answer, even if it's as plain as can be to everyone else. But when we look at someone else's situation, it's easy to diagnose the answer. Likewise, sometimes it can be easier to have faith and believe *for someone else* than *for yourself.* That's worth repeating: Sometimes it's easier to believe for someone else than for yourself.

> **Father Michael:** I've seen this over and over again at the parish, especially when it comes to health-related issues or the death of family members. A parent or spouse becomes so overwhelmed by the unfolding situation that they're unable to register anything but worry, fear, doubt, and distress. They lose their grip on faith in God's goodness and mercy; their ability to turn to God's healing power is nowhere to be found. Then, into the gap step family and friends who literally lift them up, praying with them and believing for them.

At some point we all struggle with believing in God's goodness, his ability to heal, his power over a difficult situation, and his presence in a storm. We doubt that God really has the whole world in his hands, much less that he has our world in his hands. What if rather than trying to drum up more faith, you could count on the faith of others? What if you had a group of people you could text to say, "Guys, I'm currently struggling to really believe God has a purpose and vision for my life right now. Please pray that I will believe it and see it"?

This is why Christian community is so important. When we encounter obstacles, we can ask others to believe for us and pray for us. Other Christ followers can believe in God's goodness and grace for us when we struggle to believe in them for ourselves. Jesus can use their faith to accomplish something in our lives. Faith can be transferred like money between bank accounts. Likewise, God can use our faith to make a positive impact on the lives of others. You can believe for others when they cannot believe for themselves.

We have said it before: faith is personal, but it's not private. It is interconnected.

So Jesus sees the faith of the paralytic man's friends, and he is moved to do something for him. But, it is not at all what they had in mind. He forgives the man's sins. He doesn't do anything about his paralysis. Why?

We come to God with a problem, and we think the presenting problem is the real problem. God, change the toxic culture in my office. Heal my spouse's hard heart. Help me to fix the financial mess I'm in. Sometimes God gives us exactly what we ask for. Sometimes, he does not (see Day 33). Often, those surface issues are not the real issues. Perhaps the problem is internal. God wants to do something in us before he does something for us. Here's why: if our hearts are not healed and made whole, then we can find ourselves right back where we started, regardless of what other gifts we receive.

So he responds to this group's request for help by healing the paralytic man's heart and putting him in right relations with God. This creates another problem: "Now some of the scribes were sitting there asking themselves, 'Why does this man speak that way? He is blaspheming. Who but God alone can forgive sins?'" (Mark 2:6–7).

The scribes were writers of the Law. Oftentimes they are cast as bad guys in the gospels. But in this episode, they pose a very legitimate question. In suggesting he has the power to forgive sins, Jesus is acknowledging that he is God. To the scribes, this seemed like he was blaspheming.

Jesus responds to the scribes' thoughts (which he knows) with a rhetorical question: Which is easier, to make a lame man walk or to forgive someone's sins? Jesus is saying that it is much easier to make a lame man walk. He should know: for Jesus to forgive sins, he had to go to the Cross. So he continues, "'That you may know that the Son of Man has authority to forgive sins on earth'—he said to the paralytic, 'I say to you, rise, pick up your mat, and go home.' He rose, picked up his mat at once, and went away in the sight of everyone" (Mark 2:10–12a).

As a result of his friends' faith, the man receives both healing in his heart and the ability to walk. That's the power of having friends in faith who can believe for you.

Reflect

What is your reaction to the idea that God can use others' faith to bring his grace into your life? How do you feel about that?

Who are the people you could ask for faith-based support when you are struggling to believe?

Whom can you encourage to lean on your faith when they are weak?

Rebuild

God, our heavenly Father,
your Son has taught me that I don't have to have faith
all on my own.
My friends in faith can walk with me
and sometimes even carry me

when I am struggling to believe in you.
Show me the people you want to be a part of my faith
journey, and help me to honestly share with them
when I need them to believe for me.
At the same time, may I be someone who can believe for others.
In Jesus's name.
Amen.

When Jesus saw their faith, he said to the
paralytic, "Child, your sins are forgiven."

—Mark 2:5

DAY 27

Share Everyday Burdens

Lord, if this is the way you treat your friends, it's
no wonder you have so few of them.

—*St. Teresa of Avila*

Read

A number of years ago, we were pulling together a few people
from the parish for a project aimed at providing expanded pastoral care for our parishioners. After speaking at length about our
responsibilities and opportunities when it comes to such care,
we asked, "So what are your thoughts? What questions do you
have?" Someone tentatively asked, "Just one question: What is
pastoral care?"

Pastoral care concerns the emotional, social, and spiritual
support the parish extends to parishioners, especially in difficult
circumstances during challenging times. These circumstances
can include struggling with grief, experiencing a health concern
or crisis, withstanding a job loss and the accompanying financial hardship, or just raising teenagers and dealing with family
drama. The list goes on and on because Jesus himself told us, "In
the world you will have trouble" (John 16:33).

We don't need a Bible verse to know that truth. Our own
experience has already taught us this. We will have trouble. And
when we do, we can feel as if we're all alone in our efforts to make
life work out. Of course, that hardly ever works out well, and
besides, it's not God's plan for us.

156

Tom: Recently, I was talking to my friend Dan, an awesome volunteer minister and overall supporter of our parish. He asked me to pray for his nephew, who aspires to be a Navy SEAL and was going through Hell Week: five and a half days of cold, wet, brutally difficult operational training. It is meant to test recruits' physical endurance, mental discipline, and pain tolerance as well as their overall attitude and ability. Dan went on to say that a major aspect of the training is teamwork, forcing each recruit to count on their fellow recruits. They teach them that you will not get through the training or successfully accomplish your mission as a SEAL without help. Apparently, Hell Week doesn't just test who has the mental and physical toughness to be a SEAL but also who can be counted on to support their teammates.

In Paul's letter to the Galatians he writes, "Bear one another's burdens, and so you will fulfill the law of Christ. For if anyone thinks he is something when he is nothing, he is deluding himself" (Galatians 6:2–3). We all carry burdens, and Paul teaches us that if we think we can handle them on our own, we are deceiving ourselves. If Navy SEALs need to learn to rely on one another in order to succeed, so do we. The law of Christ is to love and care for one another, bearing the burdens of life together.

Father Michael: This is why a small faith community is so necessary to rebuilding our Catholic faith. At Sunday Mass, even in a small parish, it just isn't possible or practical for everyone to know the burdens you're carrying. It's likewise impossible for you to know everyone else's burdens. I like to say that in church you sit in rows and I talk to you, while in small group you sit in a circle, and it's your turn to talk.

Groups are to be a place where we can share our regrets and relieve the burden of past sins. One small group member wrote, "For twenty years I've been filled with shame over my abortion. I was weighed down with the burden of this secret until coming to Nativity and opening myself up to the hope of healing. After getting to know my small group for a while, I felt safe sharing my secret with them, thereby embracing the miraculous healing that God wanted for me. I can now move forward in my life and help others who are experiencing this pain while feeling a new freedom I had come to think I would never know again."

In a small faith community, you can form bonds that can serve you well when the major problems of life hit, as they inevitably do. You already have a network of people who can support you and bear the burden with you. Another parishioner writes, "I joined a small group because I was new to Nativity and just wanted to make some friends. And I did! I've made lifelong friends. But little did I know that they would become my lifeline and support system after my husband was diagnosed with cancer. I don't know what I would have done without them."

And in between the burdens of the past and the potential problems ahead, there's just life, the vast expanse of ordinary time that we spend most of our time in. With the daily challenges we all face, who is with you? Who's providing *your* pastoral care? Perhaps all of this can be summarized by our friend Mark, who writes:

> From the first moments of my first men's small group, I finally realized I was not alone, that my problems, my shortcomings, and my sins were no more complex or uncommon than those of the men sitting around me. It has been almost seven years since that first day. We are still together, not just in our small groups but now as true friends and brothers who have dealt with some of life's greatest challenges: the passing of family members, severe illness, troubled teens, children becoming adults, job losses,

and more. But we have also shared many joys: new
jobs, graduations, marriages, and births.

Traditionally, pastoral care was considered the province of
clergy and religious, beyond the purview of the parishioners.
With the dramatic decline in the number of priests and nuns in
recent times, this approach has become unsustainable for most
parish staffs, sometimes leaving parishioners feeling neglected.
But the truth is, as St. Paul reminded the Galatians, pastoral care
is the business of the whole parish, and it can actually happen in
small groups. We like to say small groups are our delivery system
for pastoral care.

Perhaps you're already in a small group. If so, we hope this
week has helped you grow in appreciation of it and reinforce
your commitment to it. If you are not in a group, we hope we've
sold you on them, and we invite you to consider a few options.

Should your parish have a small group program in place—
more and more parishes do—learn all about it and consider getting involved. Even giving it a try with a limited commitment
can be worthwhile.

Of course, many parishes don't have groups. If that's the case
for you, talk to your pastor. With his permission, you can definitely put a group together yourself. Identify a few parishioners
who are open to meeting and start meeting! If you do not know
how to get started, we provide small group resources on our website at www.churchnativity.com. There's also plenty of content on
our website, and elsewhere online, that can form the foundation
of your small group discussions.

In this digital age, it is also quite possible to join a small
group program in another parish elsewhere, connecting with
people across the country and around the world. You are most
welcome to join one of our small groups here at Nativity. Online
groups include members from virtually everywhere. You can go
to www.churchnativity.com/groups/ to learn more.

However you choose to do it, commit to connect with other Christ followers in a group. It will lessen your burdens and double your joy in the Lord. It all comes down to a single, simple question: Whom are you doing life with?

Reflect

What's the difference between sharing our pain and problems and complaining?

What burdens are you carrying right now? How would sharing them with others lessen their weight?

After reflecting on Christian community this week, what action step do you need to take?

Rebuild

God, our heavenly Father,
thank you that you send people into my life
to share my burdens. I do not have to carry them all alone.
May I always know the healing remedy of your kindness,
through the love and care of others.
In Jesus's name.
Amen.

Bear one another's burdens, and so you will
fulfill the law of Christ.
For if anyone thinks he is something when he
is nothing, he is deluding himself.

—Galatians 6:2–3

DAY 28

Get to Know the Angels and the Saints

I will spend my heaven doing good on earth.

—St. Thérèse of Lisieux

Read

Second Kings tells an interesting story about the prophet Elisha. He made enemies with a foreign king named Ben-Hadad. The king decided he wanted to arrest Elisha and probably execute him after that. He sent out an army against the prophet, including powerful and terrifying chariots. They surrounded Elisha's home. Here's what happened: "Early the next morning, when the servant of the man of God arose and went out, he saw the force with its horses and chariots surrounding the city. 'Alas!' he said to Elisha. 'What shall we do, my lord?' Elisha answered, 'Do not be afraid. Our side outnumbers theirs'" (2 Kings 6:15–16).

The prophet's assertion obviously didn't seem to make any sense. It was only Elisha and his servant against literally an army of soldiers and charioteers. But then Elisha prayed, "'O LORD, open his eyes, that he may see.' And the LORD opened the eyes of the servant, and he saw that the mountainside was filled with fiery chariots and horses around Elisha" (2 Kings 6:17).

As the story unfolds, the fiery chariots incapacitate the invading army, driving them away, although they do extend considerable mercy toward them too. Clearly Elisha rightly recognized another reality, a higher reality, and in recognizing that reality, he was able to see the great host who surrounded him.

As we noted at the beginning of the week, we can sometimes feel like Elisha's servant. We're surrounded by a culture that seems indifferent and even at times hostile to our faith. It may feel as if you're the only Christian in your workplace, family, or neighborhood. This is why you need a local parish and can benefit so much from a commitment to a small, faith-sharing group.

You need people who can physically walk with you, but we would be remiss if we didn't remind you that the Church and its community extend beyond this world you can see. Our faith teaches us about the supernatural community that stands in and beyond this world. The book of Hebrews says, "Therefore, since we are surrounded by so great a cloud of witnesses, let us rid ourselves of every burden and sin that clings to us and persevere in running the race that lies before us while keeping our eyes fixed on Jesus, the leader and perfecter of faith" (Hebrews 12:1-2). These words from Hebrews follow a list of Old Testament heroes, from Noah to Abraham to Moses and many others (Hebrews 11). They aren't just outstanding ancients whose stories we tell over and over again. Hebrews suggests they are still with us.

And that is just the heroes of the Old Testament. Throughout scripture, we read about still other spiritual beings too. Perhaps most spectacularly, in the Christmas story:

> And suddenly there was a multitude of the heavenly
> host with the angel, praising God and saying:
>
> "Glory to God in the highest" (Luke 2:13-14).

The choirs of angels are spiritual beings whose principal role is to attend to God. But we can turn to and rely on angels for comfort and protection. Scripture refers to what are traditionally called "guarding" or "guardian" angels (Matthew 18:10) who are assigned to particular individuals to look out for us in ways we can scarcely appreciate.

In the book of Revelation we read about others:

> After this I had a vision of a great multitude, which
> no one could count, from every nation, race, people,
> and tongue. They stood before the throne and before
> the Lamb, wearing white robes and holding palm
> branches in their hands. They cried out in a loud voice:
>
> "Salvation comes from our God." (Revelation 7:9–10)

This is the Communion of Saints, also called the Church Triumphant because these men and women have already, and successfully, met the challenge that is this life and are now at home in heaven. And, as we run the race of faith, whether we know it or not, we're actually cheered on by this great company.

> **Tom:** My wife, Mia, ran the Marine Corps Marathon
> in Washington, DC, a few years ago. While com
> pletely grueling, she recounted how incredible it
> was to be cheered on by people along the course
> throughout the race. Each time she encountered
> another cheering section, she experienced a
> fresh burst of energy to keep going.

Like Elisha's prayer for his servant, we can pray for eyes of faith or spiritual sight to really see all our cheerleaders. At the same time, we can intentionally seek out relationships with the saints who have gone before us in faith. They are our older brothers and sisters in Christ whom we can admire and look up to just as younger siblings look up to older ones. It is true that from place to place and time to time the saints have been celebrated to the point that they lose their humanity and veneration becomes worship. Our faith calls us to worship God and God alone. The saints are real-life, flesh-and-blood Christ followers. As we get to know them, we can learn from their faults and failures as well as their heroic accomplishments.

Perhaps your own life experiences can suggest saints you could get to know better. Both of us went to Jesuit schools, and so naturally we have formed admiration and devotion to the Jesuit founder, St. Ignatius Loyola. We especially appreciate him as a sort of spiritual entrepreneur, helping to renew and restore the Church during a period of disruption. He established a religious order that quickly had and continues to have a worldwide impact. We consider ourselves students of Ignatius and have sought to learn from him over the years.

Perhaps another place to get started with the saints is your own name, if you are named after a saint.

> **Tom:** There are many Thomases in the Communion of Saints, so I have my pick. As a kid I liked Thomas More for a very kidlike reason: namely, because I thought it was cool that he was beheaded. In first grade, when asked to draw a picture of my patron saint, I drew a stick figure with a head detached from its body. (I think my mom actually still has that drawing.) Such is the mind of a first-grade boy. As I have grown up, my admiration for Thomas has matured just a bit. As a husband and father, I can appreciate his loyalty to his family and his love for his daughter. I admire his razor-sharp wit and his incredible integrity. At the same time, I have been encouraged to learn about his personal struggles, many of which I share.

> **Father Michael:** I have always been inspired by the archangel Michael, whose name means "Who is like God?" It's a question challenging the devil, who wished to overtake God's authority. It is a rebuke and a reminder of our need for humility. Michael represents a heroic humility, a quality I esteem and aspire to emulate.

Through our Baptism, in our prayer and worship, and most of all at Holy Mass, we are united to the company of angels and saints in heaven. But we can live our everyday life in their company too.

Mary, Mother of God

However, it is not only the angels and saints whom we are united to in faith. From the Cross, Jesus himself directs our attention to his mother, Mary. While on the Cross, "when Jesus saw his mother and the disciple there whom he loved, he said to his mother, 'Woman, behold, your son.' Then he said to the disciple, 'Behold, your mother'" (John 19:26–27). In that moment, he directed all those who have faith in him to look upon her as our mother.

Tradition tells us she held a revered place among the apostles and in the life of the early church. As it grew, Marian devotion distinguished the life of the whole Church, East and West, with dedicated feast days appearing as early as the third and fourth centuries. Local and regional devotions sprung up among the faithful in many places, and the consecration of churches and chapels in her honor became widespread. Those early patterns eventually characterized the life and pious practices of the Catholic Church everywhere.

Mary's role is critical to understand when it comes to renewing or rebuilding our Catholic faith. As Catholics we do not pray to Mary; we pray through Mary to Jesus. She is the first and perfect disciple of Christ and our reliable guide, always pointing us to her son. At the same time, she stands as a powerful mediator, always interceding for us with her son.

Reflect

Why do you think it is helpful to see ourselves as enjoying fellowship with the saints?

Is there a biblical hero or saint whom you admire or whose story has resonated with you? What can you do to know their story better?

How has this week, focused on engaging in Christian community, changed how you view its importance in our faith life?

Rebuild

God, our heavenly Father,
thank you for the communion we enjoy
with the angels and saints.
Give me eyes of faith to see the great cloud of witnesses
who are cheering me on and encouraging me
to follow your Son,
the perfecter of my faith.
Bestow on us, through the prayers of so many intercessors,
an abundance of your blessings through Christ our Lord.
Amen.

Therefore, since we are surrounded by so great a cloud of witnesses, let us rid ourselves of every burden and sin that clings to us and persevere in running the race that lies before us while keeping our eyes fixed on Jesus, the leader and perfecter of faith.

—Hebrews 12:1–2

WEEK FIVE

Practice Prayer and Sacraments

DAY 29

Practice Prayer

You don't know how to pray? Put yourself in the
presence of God and say "Lord, I don't know how
to pray!" and you have already begun.

—*St. Josemaría Escrivá*

Read

Of the five STEPS, the practice of prayer and the sacraments is
the one most associated with the spiritual life. Before reading this
book, you might not have seen fellowship or giving or even serving as spiritual exercises, but you certainly would have viewed
prayer as one. Prayer is a universal human expression, both an
action and a reaction. Surveys consistently show that even people
who doubt God's existence or deny it altogether find themselves
at some point praying. But, while almost everyone prays, we also
have to acknowledge that something in us *resists* prayer. We don't
want to pray, especially when it feels coerced or commanded.

Faith is belief in God, and prayer is actively acknowledging
him. That means prayer is basic to faith; prayer is the fundamental expression of it. To grow as followers of Christ, to rebuild our
Catholic faith, means learning how to pray and making it an
indispensable daily habit. We have to discipline ourselves to turn
our minds and hearts in the direction of our heavenly Father
in a consistent, sustainable way that is helpful and fruitful, an

established daily habit as well as our go-to response to any and every situation in life.

And that takes *practice*. We use the word *practice* very intentionally. Practice implies we can improve at something; we can get better at it. Maybe you have never thought about prayer in that way, but it is a skill that can be refined, the same way you get better at speaking a foreign language, swinging a golf club, or working out. That means recognizing we can always be growing in prayer. We grow in our ability to hear God's voice, to raise our minds and hearts, to express gratitude to God, to confess our sins, and to make petitions.

And yet, as Thomas Merton wrote in *Contemplative Prayer*, "We do not want to be beginners at prayer but let us be convinced of the fact that we will never be anything but beginners, all our life!" If you feel like a novice at prayer, congratulations! It means you're recognizing how much opportunity you have to grow.

Practice also implies a *repeated* activity, something we do over and over again. We don't pray once, or once in a while, and then we're done. For prayer to truly welcome God's presence and power into our lives, we must keep on praying and keep on praying and keep on praying. We *persevere* in prayer. This is something Jesus taught on multiple occasions, as we'll cover at the end of the week (see Day 35).

Practicing prayer also means we live out what we discover in prayer. Many times, we think of prayer as a passive exercise, a way to withdraw from the world. Prayer, however, is anything but passive; it actively pursues the God who created the world and has all the solutions to all the problems in the world, including our problems.

In prayer we can meet the living Lord who, if we listen to him, can give us direction for living. Practicing prayer also means putting that direction into action. Most of all, in emphasizing *practice*, we're underscoring the relationship we commit to through our ongoing conversation with the God of the universe. Prayer is how we learn to be in relationship with God. In prayer, we can come to recognize and understand the blessings and responsibilities, the joys and duties, involved in any relationship.

Of course, we can pray at any time and anywhere, but to grow our prayer lives, Jesus gave us some straightforward instructions in the Sermon on the Mount. Jesus said, "When you pray, do not be like the hypocrites, who love to stand and pray in the synagogues and on street corners so that others may see them. Amen, I say to you, they have received their reward" (Matthew 6:5).

Jesus tells his friends and followers to first of all avoid hypocrisy in prayer; never pray to appear virtuous. Praying on street corners to impress others is probably not much of a temptation for most of us these days, but there are subtler ways we can try and make ourselves look good to others through prayer. We can pray in such a way that makes us look holier or more spiritually mature than we really are, and the temptation should be avoided because it is counterproductive to prayer efforts.

Notice, Jesus says *when* you pray. In other words, choose a specific time. This is really key. Put your prayer time into your daily schedule, just as you schedule mealtimes and work hours. For many people, the time that works best for them is in the morning. That way it can't get canceled, and it helps to set the tone for the rest of the day. But perhaps you may find you pray best at lunchtime or in the evening. The point Jesus makes is to find a time when you pray. Get into a routine.

"When you pray, go to your inner room, close the door, and pray to your Father in secret. And your Father who sees in secret will repay you" (Matthew 6:6). Jesus says choose a *time* and then choose a *place* where you can get alone with your heavenly Father. And, as you choose the same place over and over again, it will become a more sacred space. It will become a place where you develop greater intimacy with God; it will make prayer easier.

And that's the point: developing intimacy with God is the key aim and reward of prayer. There's that promise again, the promise of rewards. Everything Jesus asks us to do, even things that are good for us, like prayer, comes with the promise of rewards. And the reward here is intimacy.

> **Father Michael:** I had the privilege once of concelebrating morning Mass with Pope John Paul II in his private chapel in the Apostolic Palace. Our small group of priests vested for Mass in a sacristy immediately adjacent to the chapel itself. At the appointed time we were ushered in. Two surprises awaited us. The first surprise was to discover that the chapel is really *very* small. The second surprise was that the pope was already there, kneeling before the altar and tabernacle. On top of his prie-dieu was an open Bible, and the pope was actually resting his hands on it. And, most strikingly, he was moaning. The pope was *moaning*. My immediate reaction was embarrassment, as it seemed we were intruding on an intimate conversation, which, of course, we were. The scene remains with me as the most powerful example of prayer as intimate conversation. Of course, the other takeaway was that Pope John Paul had a time and a place, and when he wasn't traveling, his commitment to that time and place never varied (and when he was traveling, his prayer time and place were the very first things to be scheduled into the itinerary).

While it can be intimidating to see the depth of prayer of saints such as John Paul II, it gives us a vision for prayer and shows why we pray. Prayer is about developing a personal, intimate relationship with our heavenly Father, and that means getting alone with God and away from the distractions of the world.

"In praying, do not babble like the pagans, who think they will be heard because of their many words. Do not be like them. Your Father knows what you need before you ask him" (Matthew 6:7–8). *Babble* is such an interesting word. The original Greek suggests vanity and foolishness through the sheer and unnecessary multiplication of words. You don't have to fight for God's attention. He already wants to give it to you. Don't think you have to convince him of or argue with him about your needs. He already knows them and cares about them. Instead, be intentional about your time. Have a plan for how you will talk to God. Again, our attitude and predisposition in approaching prayer are always going to influence and affect the outcome.

There is no shortage of tools that will help you pray—a Bible of course, and perhaps a Bible reading plan to help you get started and to keep you going. Spiritually themed books can have a part in your daily prayer, and many people find journaling of great practical help. Then, of course, there are prayer guides and prayer books, prayer podcasts, and daily devotionals. When it comes to how long your prayer time should be, start somewhere; start anywhere. Even five or six minutes a day can be a place to begin.

Whatever form your prayer takes, make sure the following are priorities:

- Adoration: we adore God and recognize his greatness.

- Contrition: we acknowledge our sinfulness.

- Thanksgiving: we thank God for his goodness to us.

- Supplication: we ask God for what we want and need.

- Silence: we listen to the Lord.

- Persistence: we never give up.

Over the next few days we will look at how you can establish a prayer plan, identify tools that will help deepen your prayer, and grow in your ability to pray. Today, reflect and pray on your own thoughts on prayer.

Reflect

How do you define prayer?

How would you rank your prayer life on a scale of one to five? Why do you answer as you do? What would help you improve?

When do you pray and where do you pray? How is that time and place working for you?

Rebuild

God, our heavenly Father,
thank you for the great gift of prayer
and the opportunity to enter into conversation with you.
Setting aside a time and a place
to connect with you on a daily basis,
may I open my heart to your heart and grow closer to you.
In Jesus's name.
Amen.

When you pray, go to your inner room, close the door, and pray to your Father in secret. And your Father who sees in secret will repay you.

—Matthew 6:6

DAY 30

Worship and Adore

There is no better way to experience the good God than to find
him in the perfect sacrifice of the Mass.

—*St. John Vianney*

Read

When we pray, our natural disposition is to bring to God our
needs. We pray for blessings; we pray for deliverance from evil;
we pray for health and strength. But that is *not* where Jesus told
us to begin.

In the Gospel of Luke, we read that Jesus "was praying in
a certain place, and when he had finished, one of the disciples
said to him, 'Lord, teach us to pray just as John taught his disciples'" (Luke 11:1). The apostles, as good Jewish men, would have
learned many prayers from the time they were children, and yet
they rightly know there must be *more* to prayer given the time
Jesus invested in it. So, Jesus teaches them:

> When you pray, say:
>
> Father, hallowed be your name,
> > your kingdom come. (Luke 11:2)

This passage forms the basic prayer of all Christians, the Our
Father. But Jesus wasn't only teaching a specific prayer; he was
teaching *how* to pray. Begin by praising God and recognizing
his goodness and greatness and holiness. Why is that? Why does
God command that we adore him?

Spirituality 101 is this: there is a God, and it is not you. Yet we forget that fact over and over again. We can wake up every morning as "practical atheists," thinking that the world is all on our shoulders, that if it is going to *be*, it is up to *me*. When we pause to acknowledge God's greatness, we are reminded that he is the ruler of the universe, and we are not. It's like hitting reset and reestablishing the correct order of things.

In adoration or worship, we recognize our proper place in the universe before the God who created it. He is the Creator; we are the created. He is the Savior; we are the saved. He is the Sanctifier; we are the sanctified.

On the surface it could seem petty of God to command worship, but it is for our benefit that he does so. Adoration and worship remind us that God's love comes first. We did not choose God; God chose us. Our lives and very existence overflow from God's loving goodness. For this reason, Jesus teaches us to begin prayer with worship.

So how do we adore and praise God? We can learn to praise God in a few different ways.

Holy Mass

The Mass is the source and the summit of our Catholic faith, and as such, it is the perfect prayer. And as the perfect prayer, it is the highest form of worship as well as a kind of *school* for worship. We can learn to worship at Mass.

The Mass comes in two main parts. First, we enter the Liturgy of the Word, which includes the readings from scripture and then the homily, breaking open God's Word and providing instruction and inspiration. Next comes our fundamental statement of faith, the Apostles' or Nicene Creed. The Liturgy of the Word ends in intercessory petitions called the Universal Prayer.

Second, the Liturgy of the Eucharist forms the very heart of our worship. This part of the liturgy begins with the *Sanctus*, or the Holy, Holy, Holy, reflecting the worship of the angels as related in the book of Isaiah and again in the book of Revelation. In English, we would say holy, holier, holiest, but Hebrew has no superlatives or comparatives. So when we sing "holy" three times, we are saying God is the holiest, deserving of all our praise. The second half of the acclamation, "Blessed is he who comes in the name of the Lord," is also a scriptural reference, this time to the words that the crowds used to greet Jesus in Jerusalem on Palm Sunday (Matthew 21:9). They praised him as a king who was coming to save them. In the same way, we are praising Jesus as our king as we prepare for him to come to us in the Eucharist.

Then we kneel. This too teaches us about adoring and worshiping God. As physical beings, our posture affects our prayer. By kneeling, we give physical expression to what we are doing. It is a posture of supplication, part of the work we do in the liturgy and a sign of our respect and love.

The great Eucharistic Prayer moves us to the consecration. By means of his own words and actions, the sacrifice that Christ himself instituted during the Last Supper is affected. There, he offered his Body and Blood under the species of bread and wine, an action completed on the Cross, the saving events that take away the sins of the world. Our Catholic faith teaches us that Christ's sacrifice is really made present in the Mass. And so, we complete the Eucharistic Prayer with the reception of Holy Communion. In our Communion, we receive the Real Presence of Christ to heal and strengthen us but also to restore and renew us in the image of Christ himself.

As we offer this perfect sacrifice, that is, Christ's sacrifice, it calls us to increasingly offer ourselves, the whole of our lives, as a *living* sacrifice. And so, day by day, we are brought into greater unity with God and one another.

The Rosary

Among all the prayer tools at our disposal, the Rosary has traditionally held pride of place for Catholics.

According to pious legend, the concept of the Rosary was given to St. Dominic in a beatific vision early in the twelfth century. By the mid-1500s, it was in wide use throughout the Catholic world. Essentially a rote recitation of the Hail Mary, the Rosary in fact proposes a series of meditations on Christ. The repetition grounds the prayer and makes space for actual meditation, a kind of mental lingering in the great moments of Christ's life, death, and resurrection.

The Liturgy of the Hours

The Liturgy of the Hours forms the official or public prayer of the Church, prayerfully marking the hours of each day. It consists primarily of psalms, hymns, prayers, and spiritual readings.

From the New Testament we learn that the very earliest community of the faithful gathered daily to pray together (Acts 2:46). The Church was united, first of all, in prayer. Early Christians were simply reflecting the Jewish custom of praying certain prayers at specific times of day. It was during the Middle Ages that the custom became more elaborate as it was celebrated throughout the day in medieval monastic communities.

A simplified version of the Liturgy of the Hours was eventually developed by the Franciscans for use by clergy not living in monasteries as well as the faithful who wished to join in the prayer but had obvious constraints on their time. This shortened version, known as the Breviary, contains the two principal hours (really just ten to twenty minutes) of the day: Morning Prayer and Evening Prayer. To these can be added day and nighttime prayers as well. It can be found in the four-volume *Liturgy of the Hours* published by the United States Conference of Catholic Bishops, and it is also easily available online.

The Liturgy of the Hours is intended to unite our prayer to the prayer of Catholics everywhere, the prayer of the Universal Church while, at the same time, sanctifying the whole of our day in worship and adoration.

Eucharistic Adoration

The keeping, or reserving, of the Blessed Sacrament outside of Mass to share with the sick seems to have been a custom from the church of the apostles. Reserving the Sacrament for the purpose of adoration was also an early practice, becoming more widely encouraged through the teaching and preaching of St. Francis of Assisi, St. Thomas Aquinas, and others.

Prayer before the Blessed Sacrament, either reposed in the altar tabernacle or exposed in the monstrance, can be an effective and even powerful form of adoration. The presence of Christ in the Sacrament, the theological basis for adoration, is experienced in a unique way, heightening our appreciation of and desire for the Eucharist. Regular visits to the place of reservation at your parish church or even a weekly Holy Hour can be real catalysts for spiritual health and growth.

Singing

Augustine once wrote "singing is for one who loves," and he is sometimes cited as the source of the famous proverb "Whoever sings prays twice." Music and sung worship provide perhaps the most accessible, immediate tool to help us worship and adore God. Praising God means lifting up our souls to him, and with worship music that becomes so much easier to do. No matter your musical taste, there is music that can fill your heart and lift up your soul to the Lord.

Consider singing as a vitally important tool in your toolbox. Go on Spotify or iTunes and find music you can play in the car, while you are cleaning or cooking, or as you work out or exercise. Doing so could dramatically increase your prayer time.

The Christian life, when lived as God intends, isn't a matter of trying harder, wishful thinking, or good luck. It's about the overflow of God's love into our lives. When we worship and honor

God, we stand in his love, the core truth of our being. And then our prayer, and the whole of our lives, can be a *response* to that love.

Reflect

Why is it important to have adoration as part of our prayer practice?

Do you regularly turn to worship and adoration? When and how?

As a result of this reflection, what is one action you can take to add more praise and adoration into your prayer practice?

Rebuild

God, our heavenly Father,
you alone are worthy of our praise and adoration.
As we recall the wonders of Christ's love for us,
may we increasingly be made worthy to receive
an abundance of your grace through Christ our Lord.
Amen.

O God, you are my God—
it is you I seek!
For you my body yearns;
for you my soul thirsts.

—Psalm 63:2

DAY 31

Embrace Humility

The most important aspect of the spiritual life? Humility, humility, humility.

—*St. Bernard of Clairvaux*

Read

Humility is the most important virtue in the Christian life because it paves the way to all other virtues. And nothing humbles us more than acknowledging our own flaws, faults, and failures.

We may not like facing our shortcomings, much less our sins, but the truth is that we cannot grow as followers of Christ until we repent and confess our need for God's mercy. So vital is repentance that Jesus launched his ministry with the call to *repent* (Matthew 4:17).

The word can bring negative images to mind, but it simply is about a change of thinking that leads to a change of heart that leads to a change in behavior. To repent means to identify sin in our life, determine to eliminate it from our life, and subsequently behave differently.

If you have picked up this book and read this far, in your heart of hearts you want to be a good and loving person, worshiping God and serving others. That's the desire of your heart. And it is planted there by a loving Father. But unfortunately, we miss the mark. That is actually the definition of sin: to miss the mark.

Pilots learn a lesson in flight school that is called the "one in sixty rule." If you are off just one degree in your flight coordination, after traveling sixty miles, you will be one full mile off course. Not a big deal, until it is. Fly from LA to Washington, DC, just one degree off in your coordination and you'll end up somewhere in the Chesapeake Bay. Aim for heaven and keep getting a little off course and you'll end up . . . well . . . .

We easily get off course in life. We miss opportunities to love and serve one another. Our selfishness and sin distract us from our best selves. Repentance and contrition on a daily basis put us back on the right course. It's the course correction that puts us back on our proper flight path.

Let's be clear, repentance or contrition is not about *guilt*. As we've already noted, Jesus never leveraged guilt or shame to change people's attitudes or behaviors. The only sin he ever called out was the hypocrisy of the religious leaders, who refused to acknowledge their self-righteousness. When sinners came to Jesus, he quickly made known to them God's mercy and love, such as the woman caught in adultery or the dishonest tax collector, Zacchaeus. Jesus does not want you living in guilt and shame. Beaten and bloodied, he died on the Cross to wash away your iniquity and cleanse you from your sins, freeing you from guilt.

Still, guilt is something we carry just the same; we impose it on ourselves and sometimes others do too, including others in the Church. Everyone has heard of "Catholic guilt." The way to effectively relieve ourselves of our guilt is to humbly confess our sin. It's so simple. We name our sins and acknowledge our responsibility for them. Doing so is called prayer of contrition, and it helps us identify our faults and flaws and apologize for them. Such prayer diminishes guilt.

But even more importantly, prayer of contrition gives us an ability to see where we are missing the mark in loving as Jesus loves. It helps us to see and overcome the gap in our lives between our character and Christ's character. So where do we find prayers of contrition and how do we pray them?

Holy Mass

When we gather at the Eucharist, the first thing we do after the greeting is acknowledge our sin and need for mercy. This is called the Penitential Rite, and it can be expressed in several different formulae. It often includes the traditional Confiteor, so named for the first words of the prayer in Latin, "I confess." The rite always includes the *Kyrie Eleison*, Greek for "Lord, Have Mercy," a fragment of the earliest Christian liturgical expression, with roots in the Old and New Testament. The *Kyrie* is the most basic of all prayers, the prayer Jesus himself commends to us as putting us in right relationship with God (Luke 18:13–14).

The Psalms

The book of Psalms is an anthology of 150 religious hymns found in the Old Testament. They come in different types, the most common being the individual lament. In the lament, the psalmist, and by extension the reader, acknowledges what is regretted and offers a plea for divine assistance, usually ending in expressions of confidence in God's mercy. One of the most famous psalms of lament, illustrating this formula exactly, is Psalm 51. King David wrote it after the prophet Nathan confronted him about his sins. The king had committed adultery with his neighbor, Bathsheba, and then orchestrated the murder of her husband Uriah. It is a heartfelt prayer, the perfect prayer of contrition:

> Have mercy on me, God,
>> in accord with your merciful love;
> in your abundant compassion
>> blot out my transgressions. (Psalm 51:3)

The Examination of Conscience

Sin is an offense against reason, truth, or conscience that is, at its core, a failure to love. Of course, in order to confess our sins, we have to be able to recognize and name them. And that is not at all something we should ever take for granted or assume is automatically easy to do. To guard against this tendency, discipline is required to identify sin. The standards we apply are given to us in scripture (The Ten Commandments, Exodus 20:3–17) and the Beatitudes (Matthew 5:3–13) and by the Church ("The Precepts of the Church" in the *Catechism of the Catholic Church*). Historically they have often been compiled into formal lists usually called an "Examination of Conscience." Several can be found on the website of the United States Conference of Catholic Bishops.

Breath Prayers

Sometimes we can be going through our days and unexpectedly feel a twinge of guilt remembering a past sin. We can find ourselves turning over an evil thought or just saying something bad about someone. The temptation in those moments is to beat ourselves up, to feel bad and sad. Instead, we can actually use such occasions to turn to God in prayer, repeating the prayer of blind Bartimaeus who said, "Jesus, son of David, have pity on me" (Mark 10:47).

To make the prayer more effective for yourself, consider your breathing while praying, whispering the words of scripture as you inhale and exhale. This simple exercise can slow you down and keep you focused on the goodness of God.

The Sacrament of Penance

We saved the most challenging for last. But actually, Confession is a gift. Think about it: we can go to a priest, who stands in the person of Christ, and honestly, openly, thoroughly, and *anonymously* confess our sins. And then we're done with them.

Many people wonder why we need to go to Confession at all and tell another person about our sins. It is for the health of our souls, and it is essential to truly rebuilding your Catholic faith. There is something incredibly powerful about speaking our sins out loud to another person. It helps us to both own them more completely and release the power of sin over our lives. But even more powerful can be the priest's words of absolution, washing over us to restore and renew us.

The Confession concludes with the Act of Contrition, an expression of sorrow, a final acknowledgment of sin, and significantly, a promise to amend one's life with the aspiration to avoid sin. It can take many different forms; one common English version runs as follows:

> O my God,
> I am sorry and repent with all my heart
> for all the wrong I have done
> and for the good I have failed to do,
> because by sinning I have offended you,
> who are all good and worthy to be loved above all things.
> I firmly resolve, with the help of your grace,
> to do penance, to sin no more,
> and to avoid the occasions of sin.
> Through the merits of the passion of our Savior
> Jesus Christ,
> Lord, have mercy.

If you have not gone to the Sacrament of Penance in a long time, make plans to go sometime soon. If you only go infrequently, consider going more often or, better yet, regularly. It humbles us to help make us whole.

Reflect

What prayers of contrition do you pray now? What is a prayer of contrition you could add to your prayer routine?

Prayers of contrition help us to course correct and get rid of guilt. Which of those two benefits appeals most to you?

When was the last time you went to Confession? Should you make plans to go? What prevents you from going to Confession?

Rebuild

God, our heavenly Father,
I confess that I have sinned against you and against others.
I acknowledge my sin
and with my whole heart intend to avoid sin in the future.
Thank you that Jesus died to wipe out my sin.
May I live in the freedom of his work as a true child of God.
Amen.

Have mercy on me, God, in accord
with your merciful love . . .
Thoroughly wash away my guilt;
and from my sin cleanse me.

—Psalm 51:3–4

DAY 32

Give Thanks

The worst moment for an atheist is when he is really thankful
and realizes he has no one to thank.

—*G. K. Chesterton*

Read

Study after study shows there's no practice more effective at
increasing your happiness and well-being than practicing
gratitude.

In one study, undertaken by the University of Pennsylvania,
participants were asked to write a letter of gratitude to someone in their past whom they had never properly thanked. From
this simple exercise, participants reported increased feelings
of well-being and decreased experiences of anxiety that lasted
many months (*American Psychologist* 60, no. 5 [2005]: 410–421).

In another study, two psychologists from UCLA invited a
group of participants to keep a journal for ten weeks in which
they described everything that was going well in their lives and
everything they were grateful for. A second group was invited to
journal about everything that was annoying them. In both cases,
participants' journal entries got longer and more detailed each
week as they discovered more to be grateful for or, conversely,
more to be annoyed by. This study showed what so many of us
already know: that we tend to see what we're looking for (*Journal
of Personality and Social Psychology* 84, no. 2 [2003]: 377–389).

But we don't need science and research to tell us that gratitude and happiness go hand in hand. Our own life experience teaches it. When you are focused on the good things in life and are thankful for them, you feel better. You're probably going to be healthier and more productive, making relationships with family and friends stronger and more successful.

For all these reasons, it's vitally important for us to pray prayers of thanksgiving. Prayers of thanksgiving or gratitude increase our gratitude as we grow to be more like Jesus, who himself prayed such prayers. In doing so, we also prepare the way for prayers of supplication, in which we ask for God's help or blessing (see Day 33). Just as you thank someone for past support before asking for another favor, it's important to thank God for his blessings before looking for further help. That's what Jesus himself did before he asked for the power to raise Lazarus from the dead. He prayed, "Father, I thank you for hearing me" (John 11:41).

In our Catholic faith, the Holy Mass is the ultimate prayer of thanksgiving. While it is referred to by many different names— the Lord's Supper, Holy Communion, the Breaking of Bread— the proper title for the Mass is the *Eucharist*. The New Testament was written in Greek, and the Greek noun *Eucharist*—meaning "thanksgiving"—as well as the verb *Eucharistasis*—meaning "give thanks"—is found multiple times.

"For I received from the Lord what I also handed on to you, that the Lord Jesus, on the night he was handed over, took bread, and, after he had given thanks, broke it and said, 'This is my body that is for you. Do this in remembrance of me'" (1 Corinthians 11:23–24). Each time we celebrate the Mass we thank God for his blessings. But even more than that, the Mass also teaches us *how* to express gratitude to God in the three principal ways we are thanking him.

We Thank God for Creation

Everything that exists comes as a result of God's creation. Thus, the beauty of a sunset, the majesty of a mountain, and the power of the ocean all speak to us of the endless creativity of God. The vastness of space reveals his infinite nature. The colorful petals of a delicate spring flower suggest his artistry. A playful puppy tells us about his sense of fun. Moreover, everything and everyone you love and appreciate about life comes ultimately from God. He is the source of all good things. We thank him for a good meal and a great time, family and friends, and music and laughter. Anything we enjoy can be a reason to thank God.

Our celebration of the Eucharist is our greatest opportunity to give thanks for the created order. As the *Catechism of the Catholic Church* teaches, in the Eucharist creation itself is offered to God the Father through the sacrifice of Christ on the Cross (*CCC* 1359). The Cross is a thanksgiving offering for *all* of creation.

We Thank God for Our Redemption

Jesus instituted the Eucharist at a Passover meal. This was not accidental but intentional, as all of Jesus's life was intentional. He tells the apostles, "I have eagerly desired to eat this Passover with you before I suffer" (Luke 22:15).

Passover remembers and celebrates God freeing the Israelites from slavery in Egypt. As we have seen, he sent Moses to demand their release. When the pharaoh refused, God sent plagues to convince him to change his mind. Despite the pain, the pharaoh remained stubborn. So God declared a final, terrible plague, the death of the firstborn in every family. God gave specific instructions to Moses to save the Israelites: they were to sacrifice a lamb and cook and eat it after painting their doorposts with the lamb's blood. Seeing the blood, the angel of death would pass over the household. Then, to remember this redemption, they were to continue this meal in perpetuity.

And so Jesus, *the lamb of God who takes away the sin of the world*, who takes away *our* sin, institutes the Eucharist to continue the celebration of Passover. The gospels tell us, "Then he took the bread, said the blessing, broke it, and gave it to them, saying, 'This is my body, which will be given for you; do this in memory of me'" (Luke 22:19). When we celebrate the Eucharist we thank God for sending his Son to die on the Cross to take away our sins. We thank God that when we turned our back on him, he didn't turn his back on us. Instead, he gave us his only beloved Son.

Sometimes, we can receive gifts that are so big, so important, that we do not know how to respond. Of course, there is no bigger gift than the gift of Jesus's death on the Cross. Saying thank you does not seem to be nearly enough, but it's a good place to start. The psalmist says,

> How can I repay the LORD
>> for all the great good done for me?
> I will raise the cup of salvation
>> and call on the name of the LORD.
> (Psalm 116:12–13)

The very best way we can thank God is by receiving Jesus in the Eucharist, where we join in Christ's own sacrifice, the only one worthy of God.

We Thank God for Our Sanctification

To sanctify something is to set it apart for a divine purpose. Through his suffering and death on the Cross, Christ has sanctified humanity. And since we too are sanctified at our baptism, we are called to be holy (1 Corinthians 1:2). God sanctifies us and calls us to holiness, transforming us into the best version of ourselves he has in mind. But, for that to happen, as with any kind of transformation, we will be tested. Jesus knew this better than anyone. In the Bible we read, "Son though he was, he learned

obedience from what he suffered; and when he was made perfect, he became the source of eternal salvation for all who obey
him" (Hebrews 5:8–9).

God uses trials, tribulations, and even troubles to purify and
perfect us. Your struggles can actually serve a purpose in God's
plan. That may sound strange, but it is absolutely a game changer
if you can adopt this attitude. St. Paul writes, "We even boast
of our afflictions, knowing that affliction produces endurance
and endurance, proven character, and proven character, hope,
and hope does not disappoint, because the love of God has been
poured out into our hearts through the holy Spirit that has been
given to us" (Romans 5:3–5).

So in a certain sense, we should actually *thank* God for our
trials, tribulations, and troubles because they are testing our
characters. And character is the most important thing of all,
because our character is the only thing that we can take with
us to heaven. When we celebrate the Eucharist we celebrate our
ongoing sanctification.

Through each of these categories of thanksgiving, we can see different levels of spiritual maturity. To thank God for creation and
the good things in our lives is an elementary form of gratitude.
It's what we teach children to do. The next level of gratitude recognizes what God has done for us through Christ. This level is
incredibly important to achieve if we want to grow as disciples.
And finally, we know we are really making progress when we
can even thank God for sanctifying us through the challenges of
life that change us. This is the heart of our Eucharistic faith and
celebration, growing more like Christ.

Reflect

Over the last twenty-four hours, what is something in creation you witnessed that you can thank God for?

When have you felt grateful for Jesus's death on the Cross?

What is a struggle you are currently facing? What might God want to grow in your character through this struggle?

Rebuild

God, our heavenly Father,
thank you for your creation.
Thank you for creating me and for creating everything
and everyone that I love.
Thank you for sending your Son, Jesus
to die for me and redeem me from sin and death.
Thank you even for trials and struggles
that you are using to sanctify me and give me
a Christlike character.
In Jesus's name.
Amen.

Then he took a cup, gave thanks, and said,
"Take this and share it among yourselves; for
I tell you [that] from this time on I shall not
drink of the fruit of the vine until the kingdom
of God comes."

—Luke 22:17–18

DAY 33

Supplicate

A humble soul does not trust itself, but places all
its confidence in God.

—*St. Faustina*

Read

Prayers of supplication represent the most common type of
prayer. Supplication is the act of asking or begging for something
earnestly and humbly. For many, we turn to prayer when we've
exhausted every other possible option. Then, and only then, we
say, "Well, I suppose all we can do now is pray." Such an attitude
reveals a misunderstanding of supplication. Perhaps we make
such statements because we have experienced disappointments
with prayer. We've formed low expectations when asking God
for his intervention based on apparent failures in the past. So let's
go ahead and admit something right out front: some prayers of
supplication work and some don't. Everyone who has ever turned
to prayer knows that. Maybe prayer works, maybe it doesn't; who
really knows, right?

We've held that attitude toward prayer too. But let us also
acknowledge that is a pretty blasé, if not cynical, attitude. We
would not take that approach toward anything else we cared
about deeply. In every area of life where we've achieved success, we did not just accept past failures; we learned *from* them,
worked *through* them, and figured out why what we were doing
wasn't working.

Let's admit one other attitude we have toward prayer, especially prayers of supplication: Sometimes, we would rather that our prayers *didn't* matter all that much. Because if prayer doesn't really matter, if it's just what our grandmothers do instead of worry, then we're off the hook when it comes to prayer.

But that's not reality. God takes us seriously. He wants us to mature when it comes to prayer in the same way that parents teach their kids about finances or personal grooming so that they can take responsibility for themselves. Because prayer is such a powerful tool, God wants us to mature in prayer. We are to learn to recognize the power and effect our prayer can have and the dynamic partnership we can enjoy with him through prayer in bringing his grace and goodness to the world.

There are a few reasons prayers of supplication may *not* work.

One reason is we're asking for something that is outside God's will. God tells us no because he doesn't contradict himself. So if we pray for something that is inherently evil or just plain unhelpful, then it won't happen by God's grace.

The second reason our prayer might seem ineffective is because the answer isn't no at all; it's "not yet." God says *wait*. In these cases, we are in God's *will* but we are not in his *timing*. There can be many reasons why we're not in his timing, but often it is because we need to grow into the blessings God wants to give us. Our character has to develop so that we can handle the blessings that are ahead; without that growth we would mishandle them.

The third reason we do not see our prayers bear fruit is that they're being opposed by dark spiritual forces. We are, all of us, whether we know it or not, in a spiritual battle. There are fallen angels and, quite honestly, wicked people who choose to fight against God and his people. God could choose to overwhelm them, and one day that will happen, but not yet. And until that day comes, these forces will stand in the way of some of our prayers.

Undoubtedly some prayers don't affect their desired outcomes. But that is not to say prayer doesn't work. Even when we don't get what we want, prayer is still *affecting us*. God's power comes through, and we really can appreciate it if we're on the lookout for it.

But it is also most certainly the case that prayer of supplication affects exactly what it proposes, more often than we might realize. The stories of scripture show over and over again instances of God responding to the prayers of his people. Just to name a few:

- Hannah, the mother of the prophet Samuel, begging for a child (1 Samuel 1:11)

- David in prayer preparing for his battle with Goliath (1 Samuel 17:45)

- Nehemiah praying for favor before the king (Nehemiah 1)

In addition to stories from scripture, there are also examples happening today. Allow us to share one story where God's power came through in a mighty and miraculous way here at our parish.

> **Tom:** One of our parishioners, Andrea, had a fairly serious medical procedure that went horribly wrong, leaving her in constant and intense pain. She could barely function at all, much less fulfill her responsibilities as a mother of five. Her doctor said there was nothing he could do for her. All the specialists agreed. Unanswered prayer? Not quite. Eventually, she heard about our healing prayer team here at church. The team prayed for Andrea; they prayed with her, they prayed over her, and they prayed intensely over her area of greatest pain. After their very first session, she began to feel better. Today she is completely free from pain to the amazement of her medical team. God heard their prayer and answered with a miracle.

Rather than focus on failed prayers of supplication, which is easy to do, we need to learn more from our wins. The success stories of prayer are undeniable. We need to acknowledge that so we can grow to be more effective in prayer.

Here are some things we have learned through the years about how to make our prayers of supplication more effective.

Approach God with specifics. Put very specific requests before God. The problem with vague prayers is that we don't really know if God has answered them. When you say a blessing over your food, how do you know if God actually blessed it? It tastes the same. When we pray "bless our travels and protect me from harm," how do we know God protected us? Maybe you're just a really good driver. God wants to be known. He wants to reveal himself to us, and so it is only through specific prayers that we can really see God's power and presence. So, don't just pray for your children to be blessed, pray that they will find good friends at school. Instead of praying for your job, pray God will give you the answer to a difficult problem you've been facing. Instead of praying for the poor, ask God to show you which charity he wants you to help.

Approach God with confidence and humility. Hebrews says, "Let us confidently approach the throne of grace to receive mercy and to find grace for timely help" (Hebrews 4:16). Confident prayers express faith and hope. Pray confidently. But, at the same time, come to him humbly (see Day 31). Our prayers should not be demanding or filled with any sense of entitlement, but instead they should simply acknowledge that he does not owe us anything. We are asking for his grace and favor but also for his will to be done. Jesus modeled this for us in the Garden of Gethsemane. He prayed that the cup of suffering would be taken away from him, but he also prayed that not his will but the Father's will be done.

Approach God with others. There's definitely power in praying for and with others, as Andrea's story compellingly illustrates. Jesus said where two or three are gathered he is there with us (Matthew 18:20). Andrea was healed in the context of a whole team of parishioners that were praying for her. The bigger the prayer, the more people you want praying for you.

Reflect

When have you been disappointed that prayer did not seem to make a difference?

Have you ever experienced a clear answer to prayer? If so, what was it?

What can you specifically pray for today?

Rebuild

God, our heavenly Father,
thank you for inviting me to bring to you my needs.
I believe that you hear my prayer and know my every need.
May I grow to approach you both humbly and confidently,
seeing your hand ever more clearly each day.
Amen.

David answered him: "You come against me with sword and spear and scimitar, but I come against you in the name of the LORD of hosts, the God of the armies of Israel whom you have insulted."

—1 Samuel 17:45

DAY 34

Listen

Prayer is the raising of the mind to God. We must always
remember this. The actual words matter less.

—*St. John XXIII*

Read

Jesus calls himself the good shepherd who goes before his sheep.
He calls out to them, and they follow him (John 10:3–4, 11–16).
Often, shepherds would share a communal pen for their sheep
where they could be kept safe at night. When morning came,
the shepherd would walk through the pen with his own special
call for his sheep, who would follow him out of the pen. Mean-
while, the other sheep would stay put, waiting for the call of their
shepherd.

Practicing prayer means learning to *listen* for and hear the
voice of our shepherd. So how do we know when we have heard
from God?

> **Tom:** Not long ago I needed to buy a car. It
> was not a good time to buy; cars were expen-
> sive. But I learned a friend of mine was selling
> his SUV, and for a number of reasons, it made
> perfect sense for me to buy it.
>
> I test-drove the car with another friend
> who knows something about cars. After we
> were satisfied with the drive, we returned, and
> I turned the engine off. But then, on a whim,

197

my friend asked me to turn it back on, and it wouldn't start. He said, "There's your sign." The car had been sitting for a while and I knew it needed a new battery, so I didn't think much of the comment.

I told my wife what had happened and she asked me, "Did you pray about it? Did you ask for a sign?" I answered, "Yes, of course," but that wasn't quite true. I hadn't really prayed, and I certainly didn't ask for a sign because I didn't think I needed one. It was obvious what I should do. Sensing my insincerity, she simply said, "Pray for a sign."

So I did, asking God for a sign to confirm I should buy the car. While it's strange to say, eventually I got this strong impression that God was saying, "I already *gave* you a sign." In my own understanding, buying the car just made sense. But I was hearing from God that I needed to trust in him. A verse of scripture that I love came instantly to mind:

> Trust in the LORD with all your heart,
>   on your own intelligence do not rely;
> In all your ways be mindful of him,
>   and he will make straight your paths.
>   (Proverbs 3:5–6)

Anyway, I didn't buy that car.

Father Michael: I have my own story. At one particularly low point early on in my time at the parish, after our original staff was gone and after we had even parted company with some subsequent hires, I swore off hiring anyone. I was done. I had gotten to the point where I would rather work alone and try to do everything myself or leave it undone than deal again with the heartbreak of wrecked staff relationships.

This resolve of mine was formed, coincidently, just as Tom had met someone who he thought would be a perfect fit for us. I refused to interview the guy, even though we desperately needed the help. Tom continued to lobby, and I continued to resist. Finally, he asked me if I would at least pray about it, which, remarkably, is exactly what I had not done. I dedicated a whole weekend to prayer about developing a great staff. Through the course of the weekend cycle of Masses I raised this problem up to the Lord again and again, begging for guidance: *Why won't you give me the people I need to do the job you want me to do?*

Later, I guess God heard me because I definitely heard him. Toward the end of the last Mass of the weekend God came thundering back: *I'll send you the right people when you're ready to treat them right.* At least, I'm pretty sure that was the Lord since it was not at all what I wanted to hear. But it was so strong and so clear I set out that very day on a new course. We made that hire and, since then, many successful additional ones. Today, we have an amazing parish staff.

There are three points to remember when it comes to hearing from God.

First point: Sometimes we don't *want* to hear from God. We have our plans and our agenda; we already know what we want to do, and God's not a part of the decision-making process. Sometimes we're too busy to listen; we're too much in a hurry.

We don't give ourselves a chance to hear from him. Scripture tells us, Fr. Michael's experience notwithstanding, God is most likely going to speak to us in a voice that is "a still small voice" (1 Kings 19:12–13, *Revised Standard Version Catholic Edition*). To hear that voice, we need to slow down and embrace silence.

Second point: Fill that silence with scripture, through which God speaks to us in a very direct way. Read, reflect, memorize. Pick a verse and repeat it throughout the day. This will powerfully help you recognize the voice of the Good Shepherd.

Third point: We can also hear from God through the voices of other Christ followers. When you start hearing the same message from different reliable sources, it could be an indication that God is trying to get your attention. The effective teaching and preaching of the Church can sometimes also be a direct message from God to you. And, of course, the great treasury of Catholic spiritual writing can be an important resource as well.

Hearing God's voice will be personal, for sure. God has created you as a wholly unique individual, so he will speak to you in a way that is unique to you. As we've already suggested, definitely develop a daily quiet time, even just five or six minutes a day, that can be your time to listen as you spend time with scripture. Increasingly be open to listen at other times, anytime, all the time. You might hear God on a hike, while working out, or driving in the car. He might speak to you through music or even in a dream. But it only helps if you are listening.

Reflect

Has there ever been a time you have heard from God?

What scripture verses about listening in prayer speak to your heart?

When in your day can you cultivate silence so you can hear from God?

Rebuild

God, our heavenly Father,
I know that you speak to me softly and gently
as well as loudly and urgently.
Help me to recognize your voice
and learn to understand
the movements of the Spirit within me.
Accompany me with constant care and protection,
and so make me worthy of eternal redemption.
Through our Lord Jesus Christ, your Son,
and in the unity of the Holy Spirit,
one God, forever and ever.
Amen.

Then the Lord said: Go out and stand on the mountain before the Lord; the Lord will pass by. There was a strong and violent wind rending the mountains and crushing rocks before the Lord—but the Lord was not in the wind; after the wind, an earthquake—but the Lord was not in the earthquake; after the earthquake, fire—but the Lord was not in the fire; after the fire, a light silent sound.

—1 Kings 19:11–12

DAY 35

Persevere

The desire of your heart is itself your prayer.

—*St. Augustine*

Read

At one point in the Gospel of Luke, Jesus tells his friends and followers a strange story: "There was a judge in a certain town who neither feared God nor respected any human being. And a widow in that town used to come to him and say, 'Render a just decision for me against my adversary'" (Luke 18:2–3).

Jesus sets up two characters. The first is a judge. Judges, then as now, were very powerful people. And Jesus explains that this judge not only has power but also abuses it. Then there is a second character, a widow. She was also completely helpless and utterly alone before the judge, hardly a strong position in which to ask him for vindication.

"For a long time the judge was unwilling, but eventually he thought, 'While it is true that I neither fear God nor respect any human being, because this widow keeps bothering me I shall deliver a just decision for her'" (Luke 18:4–5). So for an extended amount of time, the judge would not help her, probably because there was nothing in it for him. But, because she kept on asking and kept on asking and *kept on asking*, eventually he gave in. She simply had worn him out. She had nothing. Nothing but persistence.

Now, as we've noted, in a parable, someone is usually us and someone is usually God. Obviously, we're like the poor widow, but then that makes God the corrupt judge, right? Well, yes and no. There is a one-to-one correlation between us and the poor widow. Like her, we come to God with absolutely no rights and nothing to recommend us to his mercy.

Jesus compares God the Father to the judge because he is employing absurdity to make his point. He is saying even a corrupt judge would respond to a persistent request; after all, we have all had that experience of finally giving in to someone because they kept nagging us. The implication in this parable, then, is how much *more* will our heavenly Father, who loves and wants what is best for us, respond to our persistence in prayer.

"The Lord said, 'Pay attention to what the dishonest judge says. Will not God then secure the rights of his chosen ones who call out to him day and night? Will he be slow to answer them?'" (Luke 18:6–7). Will not God honor your prayer? Of course he will. In your time? Maybe; maybe not. But *eventually* all prayer will bear fruit.

Jesus told the disciples the parable of the unjust judge so they would pray always and not lose heart. He knows prayer doesn't always seem to "work," and we can easily become discouraged and want to quit. But he's teaching us to never stop praying, because prayer does work. Some people pray only once in a while, or in an emergency, and then, when it doesn't seem to have any effect, they give up, confirmed in their lurking suspicion that prayer doesn't work. That, of course, is no different than picking up a guitar only occasionally, fumbling around with chords or riffs, utterly failing to produce anything approximating music, and blaming the instrument. The guitar works just as it's supposed to; the problem is with the musician. Same with prayer. Prayer works, but we have to practice it to see its power.

Prayer has the power to change hearts, to change lives, and to change the world. Prayer has the power to change *your* world, because when you pray you are inviting the Almighty, maker of heaven and earth, into your world.

Prayer invites God to get involved in the problems and issues that are bigger than us *but* not bigger than *him*. God is bigger than our financial problems. God is bigger than our marriage problems. God is bigger than our problems with our aging parents or rebellious teens. Prayer invites God into the challenges we face, to vindicate us from them or even to give us victory over them.

If there is one overriding message in scripture when it comes to prayer, it is about perseverance in prayer. Perseverance in prayer works. It *always* works, even if we don't get the answers we hope for, according to the timeline we set. As we keep praying, God keeps working on purifying our hearts and building our character.

Never give up praying for the desires of your heart. Never give up praying for your dreams. Never give up praying for your prodigal child. Never give up praying for the problems in the world you want to see solved. Never give up praying for that friend or family member who does not know God so they may come to know him. Never give up because God is honored by your perseverance.

Reflect

Has prayer become a habit for you? What has helped it become habitual? What motivates or encourages you to persevere in prayer?

What frustrates you about prayer and makes you tempted to give up? How can you overcome that temptation?

How has your understanding of practicing prayer and the sacraments grown through our focus on this STEP this week?

Rebuild

God, our heavenly Father,
thank you for your Son's teaching about prayer.
Thank you that he knows
when I am tempted to give up and stop praying.
Grant me a resilience and perseverance to keep on praying
even when it doesn't feel as if it is making a difference.
Transform me so that the inclination to pray grows more
and more.
Amen.

[Jesus] told them a parable about the necessity for them to pray always without becoming weary.

—Luke 18:1

WEEK SIX

Share Your Faith

DAY 36

Followers Fish

I command you: be strong and steadfast! Do not fear nor be dismayed, for the LORD, your God, is with you wherever you go.

—*Joshua*

Read

When Jesus called the first apostles, he promised that if they followed him, he would give them an important new role with a unique new skill. In the process, he would change and transform their lives.

Jesus, however, didn't promise to make them smarter or wealthier or more popular or better looking—none of the promises our culture promotes, which is probably not surprising. But consider, neither did Jesus promise the apostles that he would make them holier if they followed him.

Jesus told his first followers that if they followed him, they would become "fishers of men" (Matthew 4:19). He would teach them how to use the same dedication, determination, patience, and courage that they needed as professional fishermen to bring people into a relationship with him. It is an interesting fact that seven of Jesus's twelve apostles were already fishermen. Rather than choosing the prominent religious leaders or the well-educated scholars of the day to carry on his mission and ministry, Jesus turned to these hardworking blue-collar guys who labored long hours at sea. He called them to a labor of love sharing their faith.

So the metaphor of fishing has been used throughout the history of Christianity to describe the Church's efforts at evangelization (bringing the Good News of the Gospel to the world). Jesus invites us to capture the hearts of people with the truth that God so loved the world he gave us his only beloved Son. For centuries, the Church's approach to evangelization was twofold. The first strategy involved sending missionary priests and religious around the world dedicating the whole of their lives to converting "pagans." The second strategy was simpler: Catholics literally "made" disciples by having large families and then forming their children in the faith.

> **Tom:** As a father of eight, somehow I missed the memo that large families have faded from fashion. But surely the days of foreign "missions," with their echoes of colonialism, are over. Besides, our mission field is no longer around the world; it is around the corner. It is in our workplaces, at our schools, on the ball field, and in our families. In a post-Christian culture, we have opportunities all around us all the time to bring people to Jesus.

Since Catholics don't have a history of evangelization the way Protestants do, we tend to think of sharing our faith as unnecessary or even impolite. We hope to help you see two truths here. First, the most crucial way to love people and bring value to their lives is by introducing them into a relationship with Christ. When we "fish," when we share our faith in Christ, we do so to help people live better, more successful lives. Second, *sharing* our faith *deepens* our faith. It is crucial for us if we wish to have a life of significance.

To get us started on today's reflection, we are going to look at a passage from the Gospel of Luke. Luke writes, "While the crowd was pressing in on Jesus and listening to the word of God, he was standing by the Lake of Gennesaret" (Luke 5:1).

A huge crowd of people has gathered to hear Jesus preach and teach. They are so eager to be close to him that Jesus is being

pushed back toward the water. This creates a problem, leading
to this solution: "He saw two boats there alongside the lake; the
fishermen had disembarked and were washing their nets. Getting into one of the boats, the one belonging to Simon, he asked
him to put out a short distance from the shore. Then he sat down
and taught the crowds from the boat" (Luke 5:2–3).

The boats were available because the fishermen were done
working for the day. Their last chore of the workday was washing
their nets, which were then laid out to dry because otherwise the
nets would rot and tear. Jesus gets into Simon Peter's boat and
asks him to push away from the shore so that he might be better
seen by the crowd.

"After he had finished speaking, he said to Simon, 'Put out into
deep water and lower your nets for a catch.' Simon said in reply,
'Master, we have worked hard all night and have caught nothing,
but at your command I will lower the nets'" (Luke 5:4–5). Fishermen in that region fish at night, when it is cooler, because the
fish swim closer to the surface and are easier to catch. But even
so, Peter had been fishing all night and come up with nothing.
At this point, in the heat of the day, it really made no sense to try
and fish. Furthermore, if Peter were to lower his nets, he would
have to wash them all over again, no small task. Besides which,
Peter was the fisherman here, not Jesus. However, Peter raised no
objections. Even though he doesn't know Jesus all that well at this
point, Peter has seen enough that he respects and appreciates his
authority. So Peter let down the nets.

"When they had done this, they caught a great number of
fish and their nets were tearing. They signaled to their partners
in the other boat to come help them. They came and filled both
the boats so that they were in danger of sinking" (Luke 5:6–7).
Peter and his fishing partners lower their nets, and instead of
catching nothing, they make a great haul of fish. In fact, they
catch so many fish their nets tear and their boats begin sinking
under the weight.

The great catch reminds us that Jesus knows what he is talking about. He is the authority on life. We introduce people not into a *religion* but into a *relationship* with the one person who knows and understands life. We help people meet Jesus not only because he makes our *lives better* but also because he makes us *better at life.*

"When Simon Peter saw this, he fell at the knees of Jesus and said, 'Depart from me, Lord, for I am a sinful man.' For astonishment at the catch of fish they had made seized him and all those with him" (Luke 5:8–9). Simon Peter is immediately overwhelmed by the gap between where he's at and who Jesus is. The power and authority of Jesus were fearsome, and witnessing this on display frightens Peter profoundly. He instinctively wants to go back to the life he had just a short while ago, before he met Jesus.

"Jesus said to Simon, 'Do not be afraid; from now on you will be catching men'" (Luke 5:10). Jesus says something to Simon Peter that he tells people repeatedly: *Do not be afraid.* Following Jesus and fear are mutually exclusive. Jesus explains to Peter he doesn't have to be afraid because, despite his faults and failures, he has a part, an important part, to play in God's wonderful plan.

Sharing our faith, the final of our five STEPS, can fill us with fear or, at least, unease; who are we to be doing such a thing? Jesus's message to us is the same as his message to Peter: *Don't be afraid.* Don't be afraid that you are not good enough to bring others to Christ. Don't be afraid that you don't have all the answers to the tough questions. Don't be afraid that you don't know why bad things happen to good people or how Noah got all the dinosaurs on the ark. If Jesus, *the* authority on life, sends you out to fish, you have nothing to fear, because he's got your back. Certainly, acknowledge your discomfort, but don't let that stop you. Jesus invites you into an adventure, giving you an opportunity to bring people into a relationship with him.

Luke wraps up this story in this way: "When they brought their boats to the shore, they left everything and followed him"

(Luke 5:11). Peter and his partners left everything—their liveli-hood, their friends and families, and their former way of life—to become very different kinds of fishermen, answering Jesus's call to "fish" for men and women. We have the same call, though we're not usually required to leave everything behind, except our fear.

Reflect

Who introduced you to Jesus and your faith in God? What was that experience like for you?

What are your feelings regarding telling others about Jesus or sharing your faith?

How do you think sharing your faith would help you grow deeper in faith?

Rebuild

God, our heavenly Father,
your Son calls me to go deeper in my relationship with him
by sharing my faith.
May I lay aside any fears or self-centeredness
and increasingly become open to seeing how I can share
the Good News of the Gospel as did the first apostles.
In Jesus's name.
Amen.

Jesus said . . . , "Do not be afraid; from now on you will be catching men."

—Luke 5:10

DAY 37

And Know *Why* We Fish

There is no salvation through anyone else, nor is
there any other name under heaven given to the
human race by which we are to be saved.

—*St. Peter*

Read

We have a confession to make: As we reflect on the five STEPS to
grow in a relationship with Christ, sharing our faith is the one we
struggle with the most. This might sound strange coming from
two church guys. In one sense, everything we do—preaching and
teaching, pastoral care and parish ministry—is an expression of
our faith intended to awaken and inspire faith in others. But still
we struggle, especially when it comes to sharing our faith with
people who do not know Christ. One reason for our difficulty is
that, precisely as church people, most if not all of our friendships
and relationships tend to be with other church people. But the
other reason for our struggle, the main reason we struggle, is that
we so easily forget the *why* behind sharing our faith. So we need
to learn from this day's reflection along with you. Like you, we
need to be reminded *why we fish*.

The Acts of the Apostles provides the basic rationale. Written
by St. Luke, the companion of St. Paul, Acts continues the Gospel of Luke, describing the early church and its almost immediate and incredible impact and growth. In the third chapter we
learn that Peter and John healed a crippled beggar at the Temple

213

gate in Jerusalem. Everyone knew the guy—apparently he was a daily fixture begging at the gate—so when he starts walking around, a crowd quickly gathers to witness this extraordinary development.

When the religious authorities, who viewed Jesus and his followers as a threat to the status quo, heard about what was happening, they have Peter and John arrested. These were the same men who had arrested and crucified Jesus. So it looks like history repeating itself.

Acts tells us, "They brought them into their presence and questioned them, 'By what power or by what name have you done this?'" (Acts 4:7). In other words, they're asking, Who gave you the authority to do what you are doing? This is a clear attempt to intimidate and threaten the apostles. But their plan backfires. Instead, "Then Peter, filled with the holy Spirit, answered them, 'Leaders of the people and elders: If we are being examined today about a good deed done to a cripple, namely, by what means he was saved . . .'" (Acts 4:8–9).

Before moving on to the rest of Peter's statement, let's acknowledge a few things. First, Peter is *filled with the Holy Spirit*. We don't share our faith on our own. We need the presence and the power of the Holy Spirit to do it. Remember that it was the same Peter, *without* assistance of the Holy Spirit, who denied Jesus three times (Matthew 26:69–75). *With* the Holy Spirit, he is fearless before the highest, most intimidating court in the land.

Second, he pushes back and states the *context*. They have been arrested after they performed a *good* deed, which was, in fact, a *great* deed. Why? Because it attracted lots of attention and won a hearing for the message of Christ. And that was a threat to the authorities.

Like the apostles, we too live in a culture that distrusts the Christian message and, especially, the Church. That's why Christian service is so important if we want to win a hearing for the gospel. Our good deeds and expressions of God's love open up opportunities to talk about Jesus.

Third, notice that Peter equates the crippled man coming to health and wholeness with being saved. We often hear the word "saved" and think of going to heaven when we die. But according to scripture, to be saved means we are brought to wholeness in the sight of the Lord, here and now. To be saved means God's kingdom grace comes into our life and changes our life in the present, as we reflected on Day 2. We share our faith not just because people will die one day but because they are very much alive today.

Peter continues: "If we are being examined today about a good deed done to a cripple, namely by what means he was saved, then all of you and all the people of Israel should know that it was in the name of Jesus Christ the Nazorean whom you crucified, whom God raised from the dead; in his name this man stands before you healed" (Acts 4:9–10). When we do something in someone's *name*, we are using their authority and power. Essentially Peter says, "Okay, you want to know how we healed a crippled man? We healed him in the name of Jesus of Nazareth. We were *motivated* by Jesus to do good, and by his power we were *able* to do good. If you want to challenge us, then you have to come face-to-face with the fact that this man is healed because of Jesus, the same guy you crucified but God raised from the dead. Jesus conquered death so that we can live life more successfully in his name."

Peter's testimony continues: "He is 'the stone rejected by you, the builders, which has become the cornerstone.' There is no salvation through anyone else, nor is there any other name under heaven given to the human race by which we are to be saved" (Acts 4:11–12). There's that reference again to Jesus and his *name*, which means "Yahweh saves." We share our faith because there is no other way for people to know that God saves through Christ. The only route back home to God is the person of Jesus Christ. He *is* the way, the truth, and the life (John 14:6).

This can sound offensive to our post-modern, pluralistic, egalitarian sensitivities.

Does it mean we're saying other faith traditions are false? No.

Does it mean they don't honor God? No.

Does it mean non-Christians cannot be saved? No.

It means everyone who is saved is saved through Jesus Christ, whether they know it or not. In theology, this is called the scandal of the particular. It can seem scandalous that God uses such specific means to communicate his grace. But think about it. He chose a particular people through whom he revealed himself. He chose a specific time to send his Son into the world. It makes sense, then, that only through him, only through the particular person of Jesus Christ, can we be saved.

Sharing our faith has nothing to do with proving we are right and others are wrong. It doesn't mean convincing people everything in the Bible is literally true. Neither is it about defending the primacy of the Catholic Church. Sharing our faith has everything to do with introducing others to the person of Jesus. It means telling others that he died for our sins and is risen from the dead. It's about sharing what our faith has meant to us, the difference it has made. We share our faith in Jesus because we want health and wholeness and goodness and grace for others.

"Observing the boldness of Peter and John and perceiving them to be uneducated, ordinary men, they were amazed, and they recognized them as the companions of Jesus" (Acts 4:13). The religious authorities looked at Peter and John and could see that they were poor, uneducated men, nobodies from nowhere. Yet they spoke convincingly and with conviction because they were companions of Jesus. Other translations say the authorities recognized "they had been with Jesus." This is what we want people to recognize about us: that we have been *with* Jesus, and that relationship with Jesus has touched and changed us in such a compelling, convincing way that they want to be "with Jesus" too.

Reflect

What good deeds do you do that you can connect to your faith in Jesus?

How has a relationship with Jesus healed you? Do you know someone who needs that same healing?

Is it a struggle for you to believe that we are only saved through Jesus? What thoughts come to your mind when you hear Peter say there is no other way we can be saved?

Rebuild

God, our heavenly Father,
thank you for Jesus, who has saved me.
Thank you that he died for me on the Cross;
By his wounds, I am healed.
Give me the courage to share this faith with others.
In Jesus's name.
Amen.

Everyone who calls on the name of the Lord will be saved.

—Romans 10:13

DAY 38

Love the Lost

If you truly want to help the soul of your neighbor, you should approach God first with all your heart. Ask him simply to fill you with charity and with it you can accomplish what you desire.

—*St. Vincent Ferrer*

Read

Father Michael: A while back, before COVID-19, when we traveled a lot for our books, we were speaking so often that engagements sometimes overlapped. Once, we were committed to speak in Oakland, California, and the Diocese of Springfield, Illinois, in the same week. Tom flew to St. Louis, the closest airport to our destination, and kicked off the conference there while I wrapped things up in Oakland. The next day I too flew to St. Louis, which, because of connections and delays, took most of the day and into the evening. By the time I arrived at the airport I was tired and hungry. Tom had driven down from the retreat center where we would be staying to pick me up. Very long story short, our GPS malfunctioned, and we got mixed up, traveling north on the Missouri side of the Mississippi (instead of the Illinois side, which was where we needed to be). When we finally got the GPS working, it indicated that we had to course correct and cross the river at our next opportunity. Eventually, it took us down a dirt lane that led to the bank of the river, where we found an abandoned ferry dock. Apparently, the GPS didn't know it was closed.

Now, besides being tired and hungry, we were hopelessly lost as we tried to retrace our path back to St. Louis and start over. The only sign of life in this extremely remote region turned out to be a biker bar. Much to Tom's annoyance, because he hates to ask for directions, I insisted we stop. It was an authentic place, down to the dark knotty wood paneling and concrete floor. And, no kidding, coming from the jukebox was Garth Brooks's "Friends in Low Places." Pretty much the whole place froze when we walked in, so clearly were we out of place. But the bikers turned out to be quite hospitable and helpful, and we got the directions we needed.

We've all had the experience of getting lost and know how frightening it can be. We've all lost things we need, such as car keys, and found ourselves angry and annoyed in the process. And losing something we value, such as a friend, can bring real sadness. There are many ways of being lost, and they all leave us vulnerable.

Tom: Worst of all can be the experience of a child getting lost. Sad to say, I know this because it has happened with my kids more than once. And I can honestly acknowledge that it is the worst feeling in the world. A parent can feel helpless; the experience, if only for a moment, is devastating. On the other hand, helping someone else out in this situation can be the greatest feeling in the world.

In Luke 15, Jesus does something we find nowhere else in the gospels. He tells three parables, all with the same theme (as we have already seen in Day 14): the parables of the lost sheep, the lost coin, and the lost son. In each parable, something is lost and then eventually found, and all three parables end with a celebration. These parables have similar themes, but they have important differences and nuances too. A lost sheep or coin certainly doesn't have the same weight as a lost son.

Here's what happens before Jesus begins sharing the parables: "The tax collectors and sinners were all drawing near to listen to him" (Luke 15:1). Specifically mentioned were the "tax collectors" and "sinners," probably a reference to prostitutes. Both groups were collaborators with the despised Roman occupiers, and so they were the object of particular contempt among pious Jews. So you have the tax collectors and the sinners on the one side. Then you have another group: "The Pharisees and scribes began to complain, saying, 'This man welcomes sinners and eats with them'" (Luke 15:2). The scribes, as noted, were masters of Hebrew law, devoted to preserving and copying scripture. And we've already met the Pharisees, the religious teachers of the Law. The word itself means "separate ones." They saw themselves as a special class of religious rule keepers. And they tended to see everyone else as inferior before God. That Jesus would present himself as a rabbi and nevertheless associate with such egregious lawbreakers, such as the tax collectors and prostitutes, offended them deeply. They mistook his loving-kindness toward sinners for approval of their behavior.

Jesus agreed with the Pharisees on many important points, and he admired their dedication to God. He believed that their teaching and preaching was solid, and he advised his friends and followers to heed their instruction. But again and again, we also see Jesus finding himself frustrated with them, and that frustration often led to conflict. He knew that as teachers of the Law they had the position and the potential for good and great impact in the community. Instead, they stood apart and in judgment of everyone else. In this sense they were as lost to God's real purpose and plan as the sinners and tax collectors—perhaps more so, because they didn't even *know* they were lost.

We use the word "lost" because Jesus did. It is not meant to be pejorative; it's meant to be descriptive of anyone—tax collector, sinner, or Pharisee—who has wandered far from God. Jesus came to change that, as he announced elsewhere: "The Son of Man has come to seek and to save what was lost" (Luke 19:10). Why did he do that? Because he loves the lost. And as his followers, we are called to do the same.

Reflect

Do you tend to get annoyed or angry at people who are lost, or do you have compassion for them?

Who is one person you know that you would describe as "lost"?

What would it look like for you to love the lost? How can you specifically love the one person whom you described as lost?

Rebuild

God, our heavenly Father,
your Son has called me to love the lost.
Save me from any self-righteousness or anger
when it comes to people who are far from you.
I repent of that self-righteousness and seek to join your Son
on his mission to seek and to save all people.
In Jesus's name.
Amen.

For the Son of Man has come to seek
and to save what was lost.

—Luke 19:10

DAY 39

Take Responsibility

Many, many people hereabouts are not becoming Christians for one reason only, there is nobody to make them Christians.

—*St. Francis Xavier*

Read

The Pharisees grumble and complain that Jesus welcomes and accepts sinners, so Jesus goes on to tell a parable.

When we hear the word *parable*, it sounds like a kind of homespun story that can apply to anyone, and indeed it is. In our Western mindset, we think more in syllogisms and logic to convey truth. The Middle Eastern approach at that time was very different. It used stories to teach truths and make arguments. And when well crafted, a parable might have multiple layers of meaning. Jesus's parables are the work of a genius, in which can be found deep nuance and dense complexity. One parable went like this: "What man among you having a hundred sheep and losing one of them would not leave the ninety-nine in the desert and go after the lost one until he finds it?" (Luke 15:4).

This parable begins with a question. Since Jesus is addressing the Pharisees, this is a question for them. He invites them to consider how it would feel to be a shepherd. That was funny because not only were the Pharisees *not* shepherds but also they looked down on them. They despised shepherds. According to their law, it was a proscribed occupation; no pious Jew could take it up. Working as a shepherd would automatically violate dozens of religious rules and laws, such as keeping the Sabbath or maintaining ritual cleanliness. It just couldn't be done, so shepherds were outcasts.

Jesus is deliberately using an illustration that would never have been part of the Pharisees' experience. Why would he do that? Jesus is teaching them about their real roles as leaders of the Jewish community. In the books of both the prophets Ezekiel and Jeremiah, religious leaders are compared to shepherds because it was their responsibility to do what shepherds do: provide protection, direction, and provision for their "flocks" (Ezekiel 34 and Jeremiah 23). That is exactly what the Pharisees should have been doing and exactly what they were *not* doing. Instead, they were only all about religious rule keeping. Due to that approach, they were losing people.

When you lose something, how should you feel? *Responsible.*

The shepherd in the story leaves the ninety-nine in the wilderness and goes looking for the lost sheep because he knows he is responsible for it. Sheep are known to wander off, so that part of the story is no surprise; that is precisely why sheep *need* a shepherd. To this we might think, Isn't he responsible for the other ninety-nine? Yes, but a shepherd of such a large flock would likely have had an assistant.

Jesus continues the parable, "And when he does find it, he sets it on his shoulders with great joy and, upon his arrival home, he calls together his friends and neighbors and says to them, 'Rejoice with me because I have found my lost sheep'" (Luke 15:5–6).

When sheep get lost, they become completely helpless, eventually unable to move at all. If it is not found and literally carried back to the flock, it will die. It is a mark of the strength, courage, and character of the shepherd that he rejoices when he finds it. The sacrifice of the shepherd saves the life of the sheep. In the parable, when the shepherd comes back, notice what happens next: "He calls together his friends and neighbors and says to them, 'Rejoice with me because I have found my lost sheep'" (Luke 15:6).

As we noted yesterday, in all three parables about something lost and then found, there is a party. And the party is not for what was found but for the *finder*. The shepherd says, "Rejoice with *me* for I have found my sheep." The party is for the shepherd himself. He celebrates because he was responsible for something and now has fulfilled his responsibility. That's a reason for celebration.

For sure the Pharisees, the shepherds of Israel, were losing their sheep. They were losing their sheep because they created religious obligations and demands that were impossible to fulfill. Yet it distinctly seems as if they had become proud of failing, as if their failure was proof positive of their faithfulness to their religious rule keeping. So it was deeply ironic that they were criticizing and complaining about Jesus because, in reaching out to the lost, he was doing exactly what *they* should have been doing.

Jesus ends the parable: "I tell you, in just the same way there will be more joy in heaven over one sinner who repents than over ninety-nine righteous people who have no need of repentance" (Luke 15:7). To repent is to let God find us and allow him to bring us home to him. Jesus says that when someone lost is "found" for good and for God, there is joy in heaven, more joy in fact than heaven holds for the ninety-nine who don't need repentance (a subtle reference to the ninety-nine sheep in the story). Jesus is essentially saying that in reality *everyone* needs to repent. So we all need to be saved by Jesus Christ, the Good Shepherd.

When Jesus picked up the Cross, he picked us up as well, placing all of our sins and selfishness on his shoulders. He took responsibility for "finding" us. We have only to acknowledge our need to be found.

And here's the thing: when *we* are saved by the Good Shepherd, we in turn are given responsibility for those others far from God. We join Jesus in his mission to seek and save the lost. Out of gratitude, out of joy, we join him in the work of looking for the lost sheep who have wandered far from God. We are to take responsibility, caring about the lost, seeking them out, helping them home, and celebrating that win.

Heaven rejoices the most when the lost return home. Being found and then reaching out to those others who are lost among us, restoring their relationship with God, powerfully connects us to the values of heaven. It is an exercise in joy.

Reflect

What have you lost that you have felt responsible for? What did you do when you realized it was missing?

How can we increase our sense of responsibility for reaching the "lost," those people disconnected from Christ?

Who is one person disconnected to Christ that you feel responsible for reaching and would rejoice if they came to know Jesus?

Rebuild

God, our heavenly Father,
thank you for sending your Son, Jesus
to pick me up and carry me home when I was lost.
Thank you, Jesus the Good Shepherd.
I want to join you in seeking the lost sheep of your flock and rejoice with you when they are found.
Amen.

I tell you, in just the same way there will be more joy in heaven over one sinner who repents than over ninety-nine righteous people who have no need of repentance.

—Luke 15:7

DAY 40

Invest and Invite

To convert somebody, go and take them by the
hand and guide them.

—*St. Thomas Aquinas*

Read

Over the course of this week, we have looked at *why* we should share our faith, and we've learned that the answer is simple: We share our faith because Jesus called us to do so. We share our faith so Jesus can heal people's hearts and make them whole. We share our faith because it connects us to Jesus in an intimate way and helps us share in the joy in heaven when one lost person comes back to God.

The *why* is simple. And the *how* is too. How do you share your faith? How do you fish for followers? How do you see yourself as a shepherd? We will give you two fairly simple ways over the next two days.

The first way, and the one we'll discuss today, we call "invest and invite."

As you are living your life, identify friends and family, coworkers and classmates, neighbors, and acquaintances who don't have a relationship with Christ and his Church. This identification isn't a judgment of them but just a basic fact: God, faith, and church fellowship aren't part of their daily experiences.

As church involvement continues to decline, everyone knows quite a few people who never had or no longer have any connection to Christ. Identify just one or two people to begin. You may start with someone who most needs Jesus right now. They are struggling in their marriage or finances. They are questioning their career choice or subject to isolation and loneliness. Maybe it's just someone whom God has put on your heart in a special way. When Jesus walked through Jericho (see Day 17), he didn't stop and talk to everybody, but he did stop and talk to one person: Zacchaeus. Identify the one.

Then do what Jesus did with Zacchaeus: he *invested* in him. Invest in the person God puts in your path or on your heart first of all through prayer. All of us can do that. Pray that the one person you identify will come to know Christ. St. Augustine stands as one of the most brilliant and influential theologians in the life of the Church. Yet he spent his early life far from God. His mother, St. Monica, prayed for him constantly. The Church celebrates her feast day the day before Augustine's feast day because we acknowledge that without Monica's investment, there would be no *Saint* Augustine.

Same for you: your investment of prayer makes all the difference. By all means pray. *Then* invest relationally. Jesus had dinner with Zacchaeus. He hung out with him and got to know him. He spent time with his friends. He invested in Zacchaeus through their conversation. In the same way, listen to and seek to understand the stories of the person you're investing in.

Invest by accepting where they're at and not judging wherever that is. That doesn't necessarily mean you approve of where they are in terms of choices, behaviors, lifestyle, or philosophy— simply that you receive them for who they are. We meet people where they are as Christ has come to meet us. *Acceptance*, not judgment, paves the way to *influence*. When someone knows you accept them for who they are, they are open to your influence and invitations. They know that you come from a good place and not from a desire to manipulate them. Invest in people, and do so in a way that shows your acceptance of them.

Eventually, not initially or unexpectedly, but *eventually* invest by sharing your own faith story, which we will talk about tomorrow. And when the time is right, make an invitation to church. Oftentimes, the best opportunity comes in some significant season of life: they're getting married, having a baby, becoming empty nesters, facing a health challenge or crisis, experiencing loss, or looking at end-of-life issues. Such times could make them more open to your invitation.

We tell our parishioners to think about an invitation in the same way you would tell someone about an inspiring movie, a great restaurant, or any other positive experience you've had. A church invitation is certainly more meaningful, and potentially more impactful than dinner or a movie, but we don't want it to sound that way. Make it an easy, casual invitation; that's less intimidating.

Of course, we need to address the issue of the *environment* you're inviting them to experience. We have to invite people strategically, which means considering the environment from *their* perspective: someone who has not gone to church in a long time and perhaps left because of a bad experience.

Think through what impressions they will have and what kind of reception they will receive. If your parish is warm and welcoming, the music is engaging, and the pastor can preach, by all means go ahead and invite them to Mass there. Greet them at the door, or better yet, come with them. Sit with them in Mass, and make sure they're not feeling as if they have to participate in any way that makes them uncomfortable. Take time afterward to introduce them to other parishioners, if they're okay with that. If they'd prefer to remain low key, by all means, let them.

But let's be honest, quite possibly your parish isn't that friendly and you're concerned your guest won't feel welcome. A *first-time* bad experience could be a *last-time* experience. Perhaps you can look around in your community for a parish that is more welcoming. But short of that, you can take the smaller step of an invitation to attend church online.

Online church is the new front door into church life. It is a comfortable way for people to check out church with minimal commitment. Do a little research on which parishes have online Mass and what might be engaging and inspiring for your guest (every liturgical style and musical genre can be found).

Here at Nativity, we have made a tremendous investment in our online Mass experience; even pre-COVID-19, we were committed to this ministry. At this point we're quite serious about our weekly broadcast and invite you to give it a try at churchnativity. com. A good online experience, over time, can awaken an appreciation of the Eucharist and a hunger for Holy Communion.

Faith is a gift, and it's given by God, not us. We can't give anyone faith. But we can help lead them to the giver of all good things.

Reflect

Who is someone God is putting on your heart right now to invest in?

What is the next step you can take to invest in that person?

What church environment would you invite this person into?

Rebuild

God, our heavenly Father,
give me a heart to reach the people around me
who are far from you.
Help me find the discipline to make an investment in them.

Give me the wisdom to know when to invite them
into a relationship with you
and the proper environment in which they can come to
know your love
and undying acceptance.
In Jesus's name.
Amen.

> [Peter and John said,] "It is impossible
> for us not to speak about what we have
> seen and heard."

> —Acts 4:20

BONUS DAY 1

Know Your Testimony

Modern man listens more willingly to witnesses than teachers.
—*St. Paul VI*

Read

Sharing our faith means we know our testimony.

That sounds intimidating, but it doesn't have to be. At a trial when a witness goes on the stand, they are asked to testify to what they have seen and heard. They share their experience or answer questions based on their expertise. Granted, testifying could be stressful, but if you're telling the truth, then there isn't much to worry about.

Knowing and sharing our testimony, the second of the two simple ways we share our faith, means being able to explain the reason we have hope in Jesus. Scripture says: "Always be ready to give an explanation to anyone who asks you for a reason for your hope" (1 Peter 3:15). It's about our personal encounter with the Lord and the story of how our faith matters in our life. People can disagree with us philosophically, but they can't argue with our story. It's just a question of why we believe and how we believe and what it means to us.

So hypothetically, if you were meeting someone for coffee, and they asked, "Why do you follow Jesus?" What would you answer? How would you respond? If you don't know what you would say, here are a few ways you could prepare yourself for that question and put into practice St. Peter's charge to us, which we began today's reflection with.

First, the *reason* for your hope might be a life change. In the ninth chapter of John's gospel, Jesus heals a man born blind. People ask him what happened to him. He tells them about Jesus. Eventually, the Pharisees find out about this and respond negatively. They don't like Jesus and reject his claim to be the Son of God, but healing the blind stood as one of the signature signs of the arrival of the Messiah. If it gets out Jesus healed a man born blind, they have a huge problem. People might begin to believe that Jesus really *is* the Messiah. So they seek to discredit the man. The Pharisees question him about his experience, but nobody can argue with his answer: "One thing I do know is that I was blind and now I see" (John 9:25).

Sharing our faith can be as simple and straightforward as pointing out what happened to us. Maybe you have been healed miraculously, such as the man born blind. If so, people definitely need to hear your story. Maybe your experience is less remarkable but no less important. As your faith began to matter, perhaps you finally overcame an addiction, kicked a bad habit, got out of debt, or put your marriage back together. Maybe you've experienced the goodness of God in prayer. Perhaps you can point to prayer times where God's presence was overwhelming and undeniable, and that's your reason for believing.

If you share your story, people may explain it away as coincidence or luck or dismiss it outright. That's okay. Their reaction is not your responsibility. You take responsibility for knowing and sharing your testimony. The word *testimony* means "to do again." When we know and share our testimonies, we experience the grace and goodness of God all over again.

The second reason for your hope might be the *truth about Jesus*. For some people, faith in Jesus just makes sense. They care deeply about the truth, and they can appreciate how the gospel stories all fit together; they're incredible but believable. As initially discussed (see Day 1), Jesus is the Lord, a liar, or mentally unstable.

Universally recognized as a sage, he was the only one who claimed to be God. It doesn't make any sense that such a trustworthy teacher would say that unless it's true. Or perhaps you look at the miracle of the Church surviving its first century of opposition and persecution. Historians can't explain it; it defies logic. The most plausible explanation for Christianity is that Jesus really did rise from the dead and establish a divinely ordained community of faith.

A third reason for your hope may be aesthetic. You have come to faith attracted to the beauty of it. In Evelyn Waugh's classic novel *Brideshead Revisited*, two university students become friends, and as they grow closer, they discover one has great faith and the other none. The atheist is shocked to find that his hedonistic friend is a believer. At one point he challenges his friend about such whimsical tales as shepherds visited by angels and wise men following a star. His friend responds, "I think it is a lovely idea." The atheist pushes back, "You can't believe in something because it's a lovely idea." To which his friend responds, "That's *how* I believe."

The theologian Fr. Thomas Dubay has written about the "evidential power" of beauty. You may be drawn to the beauty and grace of Jesus. The vastness of the ocean, the majesty of the mountains, and the wonderful mystery of space may be why you believe. Or maybe you believe because of the monumental genius of Michelangelo, the soaring splendor of Notre Dame, and the sheer joy of Mozart. Those incredible works of art and architecture were inspired by a culture that was saturated with Christianity, which they reflect. Your experience of beauty may be the reason for your faith.

A fourth reason for your hope may be the most surprising for people to hear: the *unity* and *community* you have experienced in the Church. We say "surprising" because a common perspective on faith and religion is that it divides people . . . which often it does. Historically, and sadly still today, religion can be a source of deep division and conflict. But the only true unity ultimately comes from entering into the communion of the Trinity.

Our desire for unity and oneness is rooted in the mystery that is the Trinity: three persons, one God. If you have experienced this unity in fellowship with other Christians, it can be a powerful reason to believe.

A fifth reason for your hope could be the simplest of all: faith works. It just works. It's a better approach to life and paves the way to more successful living.

To share your faith means you know the *reason* for your hope, which in turn, will strengthen your hope.

Reflect

When was a time you saw the goodness or mercy of God in your life?

Was there ever an experience when you felt the presence and power of God in a palpable way?

People are attracted to God in various ways. Which of the ways in today's reflection speak to your heart?

Rebuild

God, our heavenly Father,
lead me to a greater understanding
of the reason I have hope in your Son.
Reveal to me the times in my life that I have encountered
Jesus, so I can share my experience with others.
I thank you for bringing me to deeper faith
and that my faith will have an eternal impact on others.
In Jesus's name.
Amen.

Always be ready to give an explanation
to anyone who asks you for a reason
for your hope.

—1 Peter 3:15

BONUS DAY 2

Be Less (So He Can Be More)

Christ with me. Christ within me. Christ behind me.
Christ before me.

—*St. Patrick*

Read

All four gospels introduce us to John the Baptist and his ministry to share hope with the hopeless. So many people were attracted to his preaching and teaching that word began to spread that *he* might be the Messiah. However, the gospels make clear he was *not* the Messiah. Instead, his role was to prepare the way for the Christ. Each Advent we hear John the Baptist preach, "Prepare the way of the Lord, make straight his paths" (Mark 1:3).

We look to emulate the role of John the Baptist. We follow the Lord, of course, but in a sense, God also sends us ahead of his Son to prepare the way for him. Sharing our faith with friends and family members who do not know Christ, we prepare the way so the King can come into their hearts.

The final time John the Baptist appears in the gospel story comes in the third chapter of the Gospel of John. By this point, the large crowds following John have dwindled. He is no longer the rock star he was when he was first introduced at the beginning of Matthew's gospel. The new celebrity was Jesus of Nazareth, whose disciples were baptizing people now, as John had before them. Jesus has taken John's signature move and appropriated it for his own friends and followers. John's disciples come to him upset about this turn of events. They say, "Rabbi, the one who was with you across the Jordan, to whom you testified, here he is baptizing and everyone is coming to him" (John 3:26).

They feel as if their leader, whom they love, has been disrespected. Yet "John answered and said, 'No one can receive anything except what has been given him from heaven. You yourselves testify that I said [that] I am not the Messiah, but that I was sent before him" (John 3:27–28). All is grace. All we have comes from God and his goodness. John says it was by the grace of God that he could have had an effect on so many lost and lonely people. Besides, he reminds his friends, he has repeatedly taught them that he was not the Messiah and that they should expect another, who was to come. Again, his role was preparatory.

Like John, we live in a broken world. We know the problems of friends and family. We can't save everyone from all their hurts and hang-ups. But we *can* lead them to the one who does.

John continues: "The one who has the bride is the bridegroom; the best man, who stands and listens to him, rejoices greatly at the bridegroom's voice. So this joy of mine has been made complete" (John 3:29). Although John had said earlier that he was not worthy to unfasten the strap of Jesus's sandal, here he calls himself the friend of Jesus.

Think about it. There's a big difference between working for someone as an employee or servant and serving someone out of friendship and love. Not just any casual friend either, but like the groom's best man in a wedding party. The wedding celebrations of that culture were different than Western customs. While we wait for the *bride* to arrive at the church before the wedding starts, in that culture, the guests would gather at the bride's house and wait for the *groom*. The best man would stand outside the house so he could alert everyone to the groom's approach.

Now that Jesus has arrived, John's joy is complete. He's joyful that people have left him and are following the Lord. His expression of selfless joy is a sign of spiritual health and strength, a fruit of the Holy Spirit. We can be sure we're growing spiritually when we experience joy in people coming to know Christ and even greater joy when, like John, we recognize God used us to make it happen.

God wills and desires our ultimate joy and an abundant life. We follow Jesus and point others to him because he alone can lead us to such joy and abundance. The world can give us possessions, popularity, power, and pleasure, but it can't give us complete and total joy.

So John the Baptist offers his final parting words, "He must increase; I must decrease" (John 3:30). Same for us. That doesn't mean we lose our unique personality, distinctive individuality, or character traits. You are God's one-of-a-kind work of art, a treasure just as he made you. "He must increase" means that the character of Christ increases in us and the selfish, self-centered tendencies of human nature diminishes. The kindness and compassion, the strength and courage, and the wit and wisdom of Jesus must increase in us. In the process, we serve, we tithe and give, we engage in Christian community, we practice prayer and celebrate the sacraments, and we share our faith. As a consequence, we become a more perfect version of ourselves as growing disciples of the Lord. Because it truly is all about Jesus.

Reflect

What about Jesus's character needs to increase in you? What needs to decrease in your character?

As you reflect on these forty days, where have you seen growth in your faith in Christ? How have you uncovered what matters during this time?

Which of the five STEPS—serve, tithe and give, engage in Christian community, practice prayer and the sacraments,

and share your faith—have you found the most challenging? Which was the easiest for you to embrace? What do
you see as the next step in your walk with Christ?

Rebuild

God, our heavenly Father,
thank you for my journey of these last forty days.
I want my joy to be complete in your Son.
May his spirit increase within me
as I continue to take steps of faith
and so change and transform into the image of Christ.
In his most holy name.
Amen.

He must increase; I must decrease.

—John 3:30

References and Resources

Alcorn, Randy. *Money, Possessions, and Eternity*. Carol Stream, IL: Tyndale House, 2021.

Catechism of the Catholic Church, 2nd ed. (Washington, DC: United States Conference of Catholic Bishops, 2019).

Chesterton, G. K. *The G. K. Chesterton Collection*. London: Catholic Way Publishing, 2012.

Dubay, Thomas. *The Evidential Power of Beauty: Science and Theology Meet*. San Francisco: Ignatius Press, 1999.

Emmons, Robert A., and Michael E. McCullough. "Counting Blessings Versus Burdens: An Experimental Investigation of Gratitude and Subjective Well-Being in Daily Life." *Journal of Personality and Social Psychology* 84, no. 2 (2003): 377–389.

Kreeft, Peter. *Between Heaven and Hell: A Dialogue Somewhere Beyond Death with John F. Kennedy, C. S. Lewis, and Aldous Huxley*. Downers Grove, IL: InterVarsity Press, 1982.

Lewis, C. S. *The Four Loves*. New York: Harper One, 2017.

———. *Mere Christianity*. New York: Harper One, 2015.

Merton, Thomas. *Contemplative Prayer*. New York: Doubleday, 1969.

Ortberg, John. *The Life You've Always Wanted: Spiritual Disciplines for Ordinary People*. Grand Rapids, MI: Zondervan, 2002.

Seligman, Martin E. P., Tracy A. Steen, Nansook Park, and Christopher Peterson, "Positive Psychology Progress: Empirical Validation of Interventions," *American Psychologist* 60, no. 5 (2005): 410–421.

Stanley, Andy. *Fields of Gold*. Carol Stream, IL: Tyndale House, 2004.

"U.S. Church Membership Falls Below Majority for First Time." Gallup, March 29, 2021. https://news.gallup.com/poll/341963/church-membership-falls-below-majority-first-time.aspx.

Waugh, Evelyn. *Brideshead Revisited: The Sacred and Profane Memories of Captain Charles Ryder*. London: Chapman and Hall, 1945.

Rebuilt Resources

Church of the Nativity

20 East Ridgely Road, Timonium, MD

ChurchNativity.com

Nativity Online: www.churchnativity.com/nativity-online/

Facebook: facebook.com/churchnativity

Rev. Michael White

Twitter (Fr. Michael): @nativitypastor

Make Church Matter (blog): nativitypastor.tv

Rebuilt

Rebuilt Parish Association: rebuiltparish.com

Rebuilt Parish Podcast: rebuiltparish.podbean.com

Rebuilt Books

White, Michael, and Tom Corcoran. *ChurchMoney: Rebuilding the Way We Fund Our Mission*. Notre Dame, IN: Ave Maria Press, 2019.

———. *Rebuilding Your Message: Practical Tools to Strengthen Your Preaching and Teaching*. Notre Dame, IN: Ave Maria Press, 2015.

———. *Rebuilt: Awakening the Faithful, Reaching the Lost, Making Church Matter*. Notre Dame, IN: Ave Maria Press, 2013.

———. *The Rebuilt Field Guide: Ten Steps for Getting Started*. Notre Dame, IN: Ave Maria Press, 2016.

———. *Seriously, God? Making Sense of Life Not Making Sense*. Notre Dame, IN: Ave Maria Press, 2021.

———. *Tools for Rebuilding: 75 Really, Really Practical Ways to Make Your Parish Better*. Notre Dame, IN: Ave Maria Press, 2013.

Fr. Michael White is a priest of the Archdiocese of Baltimore, pastor of Church of the Nativity in Timonium, Maryland, and cofounder of Rebuilt—an organization designed to rebuild parishes for growth and health.

White is the coauthor of the bestselling book *Rebuilt*—which narrates the story of Nativity's rebirth—*Tools for Rebuilding, Rebuilding Your Message, The Rebuilt Field Guide*, and *ChurchMoney*. He is also coauthor of *Seriously, God?* and the bestselling Messages series for Advent and Lent.

During White's tenure as pastor at Church of the Nativity, the church has almost tripled in weekend attendance. More importantly, commitment to the mission of the Church has grown, demonstrated by the significant increase in giving, service in ministry, and much evidence of genuine spiritual renewal.

White earned his bachelor's degree from Loyola University Maryland and his graduate degrees in sacred theology and ecclesiology from the Pontifical Gregorian University in Rome.

Tom Corcoran has served Church of the Nativity in Timonium, Maryland, in a variety of roles that give him a unique perspective on parish ministry and leadership. First hired as a youth minister, Corcoran has also served as coordinator of children's ministry and director of small groups. He is lay associate to the pastor and is responsible for weekend message development, strategic planning, and staff development. Corcoran also is the president of Rebuilt—an organization designed to rebuild parishes for growth and health.

Corcoran is the coauthor of the bestselling book *Rebuilt*—which narrates the story of Nativity's rebirth—*Tools for Rebuilding, Rebuilding Your Message, The Rebuilt Field Guide*, and *ChurchMoney*. He is also coauthor of *Seriously, God?* and the bestselling Messages series for Advent and Lent.

In 2023 both **Fr. Michael White** and **Tom Corcoran** were honored by Pope Francis with the Pro Ecclesia et Pontifice Award for outstanding service to Church and Pope.

churchnativity.com
rebuiltparish.com
rebuiltparish.com/podcast
Facebook: churchnativity
Twitter: @churchnativity
Instagram: @churchnativity

Facebook: rebuilt parish
Instagram: @rebuiltparish
YouTube: @rebuiltparish

Bishop Adam J. Parker is auxiliary bishop and vicar-general of the Archdiocese of Baltimore.

rebuilt
PARISH

Making disciples by helping parishes make disciples.

What do you see as the next step in your walk with Christ?

Are you ready to continue your journey?

Join others who are taking steps now and rebuild your faith within our Rebuilt Community!

rebuiltparish.com/rebuiltfaith

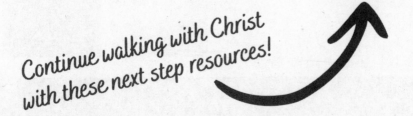

Continue walking with Christ with these next step resources!